TERRY'S CHOCOLATE® Orange

COOKBOOK

TERRY'S CHOCOLATE ® Orange

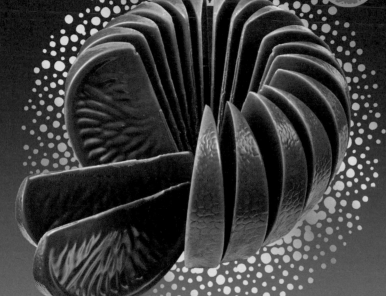

COOKBOOK

60 SMASHING CHOCOLATE ORANGE RECIPES

HarperCollins*Publishers*

CONTENTS

INTRODUCTION

We all know Terry's Chocolate Orange. It's chocolatey. It's orangey. And it's round. It's a ball in a sea of bars.

What you might not know is that it's not just good for smashing open and sharing (or even keeping hidden and enjoying alone). It's also a deliciously rich and indulgent ingredient that can be used in everything from flapjacks and granola to lattes and carrot cakes. Yes — carrot cakes.

And if you don't believe that, you'll just have to make some of the recipes in this book and discover just how good a chocolate orange can be — even when it's no longer orange-shaped.

Each recipe has a difficulty rating of one to three Terry's Chocolate Orange segments, to help you find the ideal recipe to bake.

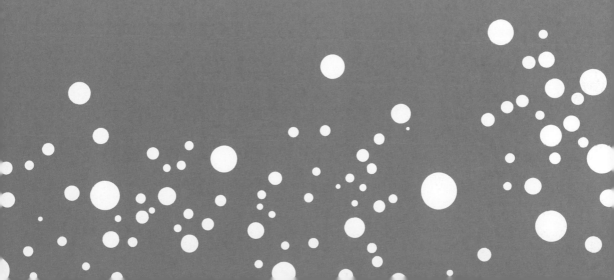

BASIC RECIPES

All your delicious Terry's Chocolate Orange recipes will go as smoothly as a chocolate fondue if you follow these basics, which make up the first steps of many of the mouth-watering delights in this book.

HOW TO MELT TERRY'S CHOCOLATE ORANGE

Chocolate can be tricky to handle for many cooks, but if you follow this method for melting the Chocolate Orange segments, whether they be Milk, Dark or White, you'll soon find yourself with a bowl of wonderfully rich melted chocolate. *See photo overleaf.*

1. Bring a small pan of water to the boil and remove from the heat.

2. Put the Terry's Chocolate Orange segments in a heatproof bowl and place it over the pan without letting the bowl touch the water below.

3. Stir the segments occasionally with a flat-bladed knife until the chocolate softens and melts.

4. You can now add it to a mixture, depending on the recipe, or stir the suggested ingredients into it.

NOTES
- DO *NOT* LEAVE THE PAN OVER THE HEAT WHEN ADDING THE CHOCOLATE.
- DO *NOT* LET THE HEATPROOF BOWL TOUCH THE HOT WATER BELOW.
- DO *NOT* USE A MICROWAVE (UNLESS SPECIFIED IN THE RECIPE).
- DO *NOT* TURN YOUR BACK AND LET SOMEONE ELSE EAT YOUR CHOCOLATE ORANGE.

TERRY'S CHOCOLATE ORANGE BUTTERCREAM

This quantity is enough to fill and top a simple sandwich cake, or to ice 12 cupcakes. You can double these quantities if you want to cover the sides as well (and maybe have a little taste of it yourself). *See photo overleaf.*

PREP: 10 MINUTES

100g UNSALTED BUTTER, SOFTENED

200g ICING SUGAR

50g MILK, DARK OR WHITE TERRY'S CHOCOLATE ORANGE SEGMENTS

1. In a food mixer, or using a hand-held electric whisk, beat the butter with a little icing sugar until smooth. Sift in the rest of the icing sugar, a little at a time, beating well between each addition, until the mixture is really smooth and creamy.

2. Bring a small pan of water to the boil and remove from the heat. Put the Terry's Chocolate Orange segments in a heatproof bowl and suspend it over the pan without letting the bowl touch the water below. Stir the segments occasionally with a flat-bladed knife until the chocolate softens and melts.

3. As soon as it starts to soften, add the chocolate to the buttercream and stir with a flat-bladed knife until thoroughly combined and the mixture is evenly coloured. Work quickly to prevent the mixture separating. It's now ready to use.

NOTES

- MAKE SURE THE BUTTER IS AT ROOM TEMPERATURE BEFORE YOU START. NEVER USE IT STRAIGHT FROM THE FRIDGE.
- IF THE MIXTURE IS TOO THICK, YOU CAN THIN IT WITH 1–2 TABLESPOONS OF MILK, ADDED GRADUALLY.
- DON'T BEAT THE CHOCOLATE INTO THE BUTTERCREAM AS IT WILL BE MORE LIKELY TO SEPARATE.

TERRY'S CHOCOLATE ORANGE SAUCE

This silky, smooth sauce is rich and thick and has the perfect consistency for coating profiteroles, using as a dip for fruits, marshmallows, cookies, pretzels and churros, or for drizzling over ice cream, frozen berries and desserts. Or just dipping a spoon in when no one's looking.

75g MILK, DARK OR WHITE
TERRY'S CHOCOLATE
ORANGE SEGMENTS
100ml DOUBLE CREAM

1. Bring a small pan of water to the boil and remove from the heat. Put the Terry's Chocolate Orange segments in a heatproof bowl and suspend it over the pan without letting the bowl touch the water below.

2. Stir occasionally with a flat-bladed knife until the chocolate softens and melts.

3. As soon as the chocolate melts, start stirring in the cream, a little at a time, until smooth. Leave for a few minutes to firm up to a coating consistency.

TRY THIS
FOR A DIFFERENT FLAVOUR, YOU CAN ADD A FEW DROPS OF ORANGE LIQUEUR, LIKE GRAND MARNIER OR COINTREAU, OR A LITTLE COFFEE LIQUEUR, SUCH AS TIA MARIA. TO MAKE A SMOOTH, SHINY CHOCOLATE SAUCE, ADD A LITTLE BUTTER AND STIR UNTIL MELTED IN.

TIP: For a pouring sauce, gradually add more cream until you get the desired consistency.

TERRY'S CHOCOLATE ORANGE FROSTING

PREP: 10–15 MINUTES
CHILL: 1 HOUR

This quantity is enough to fill and completely cover two 20cm round cakes. The addition of mascarpone and cream elevates this frosting to a whole other level.

120g MILK OR DARK TERRY'S CHOCOLATE ORANGE SEGMENTS
300ml DOUBLE CREAM
250g MASCARPONE

1. Bring a small pan of water to the boil and remove from the heat. Put the Terry's Chocolate Orange segments in a heatproof bowl and suspend it over the pan without letting the bowl touch the water below.

2. Stir occasionally with a flat-bladed knife until the chocolate softens and melts.

3. In a clean bowl or a food mixer, whip the cream until it stands in stiff peaks. Beat in the mascarpone and then fold in the melted chocolate with a flat-bladed knife until the mixture is evenly coloured throughout.

4. Cover the bowl and chill in the fridge to firm up for 1 hour before using.

TIP: You can use a hand-held electric whisk to whip the cream and mascarpone.

17

SNACKS & TREATS

Every day is a good day for a Terry's Chocolate Orange treat, from an office coffee to a quick lunchbox addition. Crunchy, squidgy, elegant or frozen, these little bites give the perfect chocolatey hit! Wrap them up as a gift or pop them all in your mouth. Yum!

WHITE CHOC CHUNK COOKIES

PREP: 10 MINUTES
COOK: 8–10 MINUTES

What could be better when you need a little pick-me-up than these delicious crunchy cookies, full to the brim with double chunks of White Terry's Chocolate Orange?

120g BUTTER, SOFTENED

140g SOFT DARK BROWN SUGAR

1 MEDIUM FREE-RANGE EGG

1 tsp VANILLA EXTRACT

200g PLAIN FLOUR

½ tsp BICARBONATE OF SODA

½ tsp SALT

1 TERRY'S CHOCOLATE ORANGE WHITE TABLET, CHOPPED INTO LARGE CHUNKS

30g PECANS, ROUGHLY CHOPPED

30g WALNUTS, ROUGHLY CHOPPED

1 WHITE TERRY'S CHOCOLATE ORANGE

1. Line a couple of large baking trays with baking parchment.

2. Beat the butter and sugar together in a large bowl until creamy. Beat in the egg and vanilla extract, then sift in the flour, bicarbonate of soda and salt. Stir until well combined.

3. Stir together the chopped Terry's Chocolate Orange White Tablet, pecans and walnuts, then add two-thirds of this mixture to the dough and stir until evenly combined.

4. Use an ice cream scoop to scoop out portions of the dough and place on to the baking trays. Add the remaining chopped chocolate and nuts to the top of each ball and place in the fridge for 10 minutes. Preheat the oven to 190°C/170°C fan/gas mark 5.

5. Transfer the cookies to the oven and bake for 8–10 minutes. Meanwhile, smash the White Terry's Chocolate Orange into segments and set aside.

6. Remove the cookies from the oven and immediately decorate each one with a segment. Leave the cookies to cool for a few minutes before serving. Sit down and enjoy them with a hot drink and a few minutes' peace (which won't last long when someone smells these cooling), or box them up once cool for a beautiful (and tasty) gift.

CHOCCY ROCKY ROAD

Sweet, crunchy, squidgy and chocolatey – this Rocky Road is a scrumptious treat for all chocolate lovers, made for those 'dessert-for-dinner' moments or when you just feel like treating yourself.

2 MILK, DARK OR WHITE TERRY'S CHOCOLATE ORANGES, SMASHED
80g UNSALTED BUTTER
1 PACK TERRY'S CHOCOLATE ORANGE CRISPY ORANGES
100g MINI MARSHMALLOWS
100g WALNUTS, CHOPPED

1. Line a 15cm square cake tin with baking parchment.

2. Put the Terry's Chocolate Oranges and butter in a heavy-based pan and place over a low heat. Stir occasionally until the chocolate has melted. Remove from the heat, then transfer a third of the melted chocolate to a bowl and set aside.

3. Fold three-quarters of the Terry's Chocolate Orange Crispy Oranges, the mini marshmallows and chopped walnuts into the remaining chocolate in the pan and stir together until everything is coated.

4. Tip the mixture into the lined tin and smooth the top with a wet spatula. Pour over the reserved melted chocolate, then top with the remaining Crispy Oranges.

5. Chill in the fridge for 3 hours, or until set. Cut into squares before enjoying a delicious bite (or three) of Chocolatey Orangey goodness!

PREP: 15 MINUTES

CRACKING KRACKOLATES

Who can resist krackolates? It's impossible to have just one, and they're also one of the easiest teatime treats of all. These are a wonderful way to introduce young children to cooking, with only a few ingredients and no need for the oven.

75g BUTTER

4 tbsp GOLDEN SYRUP

200g DARK TERRY'S CHOCOLATE ORANGE SEGMENTS, ROUGHLY CHOPPED

GRATED ZEST OF 1 ORANGE

200g CORNFLAKES

1. Place 12 paper cases in a 12-hole muffin tin.

2. Put the butter, syrup and chocolate in a pan and set over a low heat. Stir gently until the butter and chocolate have melted together.

3. Remove the pan from the heat and stir in the orange zest. Add the cornflakes, a few at a time, folding in gently until they are all thoroughly coated.

4. Divide the mixture between the paper cases and chill in the fridge until set. They will keep well in the fridge for up to 5 days.

TRY THIS

IF YOU NEEDED AN EXCUSE TO MAKE MORE THAN ONE BATCH, YOU CAN VARY THESE KRACKOLATES BY USING RICE KRISPIES INSTEAD OF CORNFLAKES, OR MILK CHOCOLATE ORANGE INSTEAD OF DARK. WHICH ONE DO YOU THINK IS BEST?

SWEET SURPRISE ORANGE BARK

Rich and orangey bark is decorated with nuts and dried fruit to make a gorgeous and tasty snack for gifting, or just tucking into when you're craving something a little sweet. And who could blame you?

250g DARK TERRY'S CHOCOLATE ORANGE SEGMENTS, CUT INTO CHUNKS

250g WHITE TERRY'S CHOCOLATE ORANGE SEGMENTS, CUT INTO CHUNKS

45g DRIED CRANBERRIES

50g PISTACHIOS AND/OR ALMONDS, CHOPPED

1. Line a large baking tray with baking parchment.

2. Melt the Dark Terry's Chocolate Orange chunks (see page 12), reserving a few segments for decoration.

3. Bring another small pan of water to the boil and remove from the heat. Melt the White Terry's Chocolate Orange chunks in the same way.

4. Thinly spread the melted dark chocolate over the lined baking tray to make a large rectangle. Drop spoonfuls of the melted white chocolate on top and gently swirl with a toothpick to create a marbled effect.

5. Scatter the cranberries, nuts and reserved Terry's Chocolate Orange segments evenly over the top, pressing them in lightly.

6. Chill in the fridge for 1 hour until the chocolate is set hard, or leave to set at room temperature for 3–4 hours.

7. Cut or break the bark into 20–25 pieces and store in an airtight container in the fridge for up to 2 weeks.

TRY THIS

FOR A DIFFERENT LOOK, YOU CAN TRY USING MILK TERRY'S CHOCOLATE ORANGE INSTEAD OF DARK OR WHITE, AND EVEN SPRINKLE THE BARK WITH PUMPKIN AND SUNFLOWER SEEDS. YOU WOULDN'T FIND THAT ON MOST TREES!

VIENNESE FINGERS

Buttery biscuit perfection, ideal for polishing off alongside your morning coffee or afternoon tea. So easy to bake, they look fancy as anything — if you can bear to share, your audience will give you a big hand (get it?).

100g BUTTER, SOFTENED
25g ICING SUGAR
100g PLAIN FLOUR, SIFTED
½ tsp BAKING POWDER
1 tsp CORNFLOUR
1 tsp VANILLA EXTRACT
200g MILK TERRY'S CHOCOLATE ORANGE SEGMENTS, ROUGHLY CHOPPED

YOU WILL NEED A PIPING BAG WITH A LARGE STAR-SHAPED NOZZLE

1. Line 2 baking trays with baking parchment.

2. In a food mixer, or using a hand-held electric whisk, beat the butter and icing sugar together until pale and fluffy. Beat in the flour, baking powder, cornflour and vanilla extract.

3. Transfer to a piping bag fitted with a large star-shaped nozzle and pipe 30 × 6cm 'fingers' on to the lined baking trays. Don't pipe them too close together – leave some space around each one as they'll spread slightly in the oven. Chill in the fridge for 30 minutes.

4. Preheat the oven to 180°C/160°C fan/gas mark 4.

5. Bake in the oven for 10–12 minutes until cooked and pale golden. Transfer to a wire rack and leave to cool.

6. Once the biscuits are completely cool, melt the Milk Terry's Chocolate Orange segments (see page 12).

7. Dip one end of each Viennese finger into the melted chocolate and place on some clean baking parchment. Leave to set fully and then store in an airtight container for up to 1 week.

TIP: It may take up to 5 minutes to beat the butter and icing sugar completely – don't stop beating before it's fluffy and much paler in colour.

MAKES 8

FREEZER TREAT CHOCOLATE BANANAS

PREP: 20 MINUTES
FREEZE: 11 HOURS

Cheeky monkeys will love these on a hot day, particularly if you don't mention how healthy they are. They're fun to make (even children love helping!) and you can add any crazy and colourful coatings to complete the treat.

---

4 RIPE MEDIUM BANANAS

200g DARK TERRY'S CHOCOLATE ORANGE SEGMENTS, CUT INTO CHUNKS

½ tsp COCONUT OIL

FOR THE COATING

SUGAR SPRINKLES, CHOPPED NUTS (PEANUTS, HAZELNUTS OR ALMONDS) OR DESICCATED COCONUT

YOU WILL NEED 8 WOODEN LOLLY STICKS

1. Line a freezer tray with baking parchment.

2. Peel the bananas and cut them in half across the middle (not lengthways). Insert a lolly stick into the sliced ends and place them side by side on the lined tray. Freeze for at least 10 hours.

3. When you're ready to make the lollies, bring a small pan of water to the boil and remove from the heat. Put the Dark Terry's Chocolate Orange chunks and coconut oil into a heatproof bowl and set it over the pan without letting the bowl touch the water below. Stir occasionally with a flat-bladed knife until blended and the chocolate softens, melts and becomes glossy.

4. Spread out the sprinkles, nuts or coconut for rolling on a plate. Dip a frozen banana into the melted chocolate and then roll immediately in the coating of your choice. Place on the lined freezer tray and repeat with the remaining bananas.

5. Return to the freezer for at least 30 minutes. The bananas will keep well in the freezer for 2–3 days.

TRY THIS

YOU CAN TRY THESE WITH MILK TERRY'S CHOCOLATE ORANGE INSTEAD OF DARK, AND FOR AN EYE-CATCHING PATTERN, DRIZZLE THE CHOCOLATE-DIPPED BANANAS WITH MELTED WHITE TERRY'S CHOCOLATE ORANGE TOO. GO BANANAS!

POPTASTIC YOGHURT POPS

PREP: 15 MINUTES
FREEZE: 6 HOURS

Nuts and orange? A heavenly flavour fusion! These pops are so easy to make and perfect for anyone who goes nuts for creamy nut butters and crunchy nut toppings.

300g VANILLA GREEK YOGHURT

3 tbsp SMOOTH NUT BUTTER, e.g. ALMOND OR PEANUT

CLEAR HONEY, TO TASTE

60g DARK TERRY'S CHOCOLATE ORANGE SEGMENTS

CHOPPED ALMONDS OR SALTED PEANUTS, FOR SPRINKLING

YOU WILL NEED 6 ICE-LOLLY MOULDS AND WOODEN LOLLY STICKS

1. Put the yoghurt in a bowl and stir in the nut butter, swirling it in until smooth. Sweeten to taste with honey.

2. Divide the mixture between 6 ice-lolly moulds and freeze for 2 hours, then remove from the freezer and insert a wooden stick into the centre of each one. Return the moulds to the freezer and freeze for at least another 4 hours until solid.

3. Melt the Dark Terry's Chocolate Orange segments (see page 12).

4. Turn out the frozen yoghurt pops by running the moulds under hot water for a second or two – don't let the water get inside the moulds.

5. Place the yoghurt pops on a freezer tray lined with baking parchment and drizzle the melted chocolate over them. Sprinkle with the chopped nuts and pop them back into the freezer for a few minutes until the chocolate sets.

TRY THIS
FOR A LUXURIOUS TREAT, WHY NOT ADD SOME CHOPPED TERRY'S CHOCOLATE ORANGE TO THE YOGHURT MIXTURE BEFORE FREEZING, OR USE PLAIN GREEK YOGHURT WITH SOME ADDED ALMOND EXTRACT? NUTTERLY DELICIOUS!

FRUITY FLORENTINES

Florentines might look fit for a queen, but they're very simple to make, and great as a glamorous ending to dinner party, or with a cup of tea after a busy day. If these are going out to a whole crowd, double the quantities and use 2 baking trays. They'll all thank you!

25g BUTTER
30g CASTER SUGAR
1 heaped tsp PLAIN FLOUR
2 tbsp DOUBLE CREAM
50g FLAKED ALMONDS
60g CHOPPED GLACÉ
    CHERRIES AND CANDIED
    ORANGE PEEL
100g MILK, DARK OR WHITE
    TERRY'S CHOCOLATE
    ORANGE SEGMENTS

TRY THIS
ADD CANDIED CITRUS
PEEL OR CRYSTALLIZED
PINEAPPLE, SWAP THE
FLAKED ALMONDS FOR
CHOPPED HAZELNUTS,
AND EVEN USE A MIXTURE
OF DIFFERENT-COLOURED
TERRY'S CHOCOLATE
ORANGE. DIVINE.

1. Preheat the oven to 190°C/170°C fan/gas mark 5. Line a large baking tray with non-stick baking parchment.

2. Put the butter and sugar into a pan and set over a low heat. Stir gently until the butter melts, then stir in the flour and remove from the heat. Beat in the cream and stir in the nuts, cherries and candied peel.

3. Using a teaspoon, drop heaped spoonfuls on to the lined baking tray, leaving plenty of room in between as the mixture will spread out.

4. Bake in the oven for 10 minutes, or until the nut and fruit circles spread out and are golden brown. Leave for 1–2 minutes on the side to crisp up a little before carefully removing them from the baking parchment and transferring to a wire rack to cool.

5. Melt the Terry's Chocolate Orange segments (see page 12).

6. Using a pastry brush or small spoon, spread the flat base of each florentine with the melted chocolate. Place them chocolate side up on a wire rack and leave until set and hard.

7. The florentines will keep well for at least a week, stored in an airtight container in the fridge or in a cool, dry place.

MELLOW OUT
BLISS BALLS

PREP: 20 MINUTES
CHILL: 30 MINUTES

No-bake, you say? A healthy energy boost? These are just the thing for when you're craving a little sweetness but don't want to have suddenly eaten a whole Chocolate Orange. Ok, let's bliss out . . .

175g DARK TERRY'S CHOCOLATE ORANGE SEGMENTS, ROUGHLY CHOPPED

2 tbsp COCONUT OIL

120ml DOUBLE CREAM

1 tbsp ORANGE JUICE

GRATED ZEST OF 1 ORANGE

A PINCH OF SEA SALT

A FEW DROPS OF LIQUID SWEETENER, e.g. STEVIA

3 tbsp COCOA POWDER

40g DESICCATED COCONUT OR CHOPPED NUTS, e.g. PISTACHIOS, ALMONDS, HAZELNUTS

1. Bring a small pan of water to the boil and remove from the heat. Put the Dark Terry's Chocolate Orange chunks and coconut oil into a heatproof bowl and set it over the pan *without* letting the bowl touch the water below. Stir occasionally with a flat-bladed knife until blended and the chocolate softens, melts and becomes glossy.

2. Gently stir in the cream, orange juice, orange zest and sea salt, then add sweetener to taste.

3. Cover and chill in the fridge for at least 30 minutes until the mixture firms up and sets. Alternatively, place in the freezer for 20–30 minutes.

4. Use a small ice-cream or cookie scoop to scoop out the mixture and, using your hands, roll it into small balls. Roll half of them in the cocoa powder and the rest in the coconut or chopped nuts.

5. Store in the fridge in an airtight container lined with baking parchment for up to 3 days.

DIVINE CHRISTMAS TRUFFLES

PREP: 10 MINUTES
FREEZE: 50 MINUTES

Christmas truffles make a wonderful edible gift to give to friends and family, dressed up with a great big festive bow. Who wouldn't want to receive a box full of scrumptious Terry's Chocolate Orange goodies?

200g DIGESTIVE BISCUITS
100g CREAM CHEESE
1 tsp VANILLA EXTRACT
1 MILK TERRY'S CHOCOLATE ORANGE
80g WHITE FONDANT ICING
ICING SUGAR, FOR DUSTING
ZEST OF 1 ORANGE

1. Line a baking tray with baking parchment.

2. Put the biscuits into a food processor and blitz until they have turned into fine crumbs. Add the cream cheese and vanilla extract and pulse to combine.

3. Using a small ice-cream or cookie scoop or a spoon, scoop out the dough and roll into 4cm balls (you should have about 12–14), then place the balls on the lined baking tray. Freeze for 30 minutes until firm.

4. Smash the Milk Chocolate Orange, then put the segments into a heatproof bowl and melt (see page 12).

5. Dip the truffle balls into the melted chocolate using a fork. Place back on to the baking tray or a plate and freeze for another 20 minutes. While the truffles are setting, would it be terribly naughty to scrape out the rest of the melted chocolate bowl and enjoy it yourself? (We won't tell if you won't.)

6. Roll the fondant icing thinly, sprinkling the work surface with icing sugar so it doesn't stick. Use a cookie cutter or sharp knife to cut out a traditional Christmas pudding splodge for each truffle. Top each truffle with a fondant splodge and sprinkle with orange zest.

SCRUMPTIOUS MILLIONAIRE'S SHORTBREAD

Millionaire's shortbread with a Terry's Chocolate Orange topping surely must be a level or two up – trillionaire's shortbread? It's rich enough for any sweet tooth, that's for sure. And make sure to use rice flour – it gives the shortbread its unique crunch beneath the luscious Chocolate Orange topping. *See photo overleaf.*

PREP: 25 MINUTES
COOK: 30–40 MINUTES
SET: 1 HOUR

FOR THE SHORTBREAD BASE

200g PLAIN FLOUR, PLUS EXTRA FOR DUSTING
100g RICE FLOUR
100g CASTER SUGAR
200g BUTTER, DICED, PLUS EXTRA FOR GREASING
60g MILK OR DARK TERRY'S CHOCOLATE ORANGE SEGMENTS, CHOPPED

1. Preheat the oven to 180°C/160°C fan/gas mark 4. Lightly butter a 20cm square cake tin.

2. Mix the flour, rice flour and sugar together in a large bowl. Add the butter and rub together until the mixture resembles fine breadcrumbs. Mix in the chopped chocolate and use your hands to bring it together. Tip on to a lightly floured work surface and knead the mixture briefly with your hands to form a ball of dough.

3. Transfer to the prepared tin and press the mixture down firmly, levelling the top. Prick several times with a fork and then bake in the oven for 20–25 minutes, or until pale golden. Set aside to cool in the tin while you make the caramel layer.

TIP: If you prefer, blitz the butter and sugar in a food processor, then add the flours and pulse until the mixture resembles breadcrumbs.

FOR THE CARAMEL LAYER

175g BUTTER
175g SUGAR
4 tbsp GOLDEN SYRUP
400ml CONDENSED MILK
½ tsp SALT

FOR THE CHOCOLATE TOPPING

200g MILK OR DARK
   TERRY'S CHOCOLATE
   ORANGE SEGMENTS

4. Put all the caramel ingredients into a large pan and set over a low heat. Stir gently until the butter melts and the sugar dissolves. Increase the heat to medium so it starts to simmer and cook for 10–15 minutes, stirring occasionally to stop it sticking and catching, until it turns golden and thickens to a soft fudge-like consistency.

5. Pour the caramel mixture over the top of the shortbread and level the top with a palette knife. Set aside for 1 hour or until it sets.

6. Meanwhile, make the Terry's Chocolate Orange topping. Melt the chocolate (see page 12), then pour it over the set caramel.

7. Leave in a cool place until the chocolate sets and then cut into squares. This will keep well in an airtight container for up to 1 week.

TRY THIS

THESE ARE A PERFECT LIFT ON A RAINY AFTERNOON! FOR AN EXTRA-SPECIAL TOPPING, SPRINKLE THE CHOCOLATE LAYER WITH CHOPPED WALNUTS, CANDIED ORANGE PEEL OR GINGER, OR ADD A TEASPOON OF SALT TO THE MIDDLE LAYER FOR A WONDERFUL SALTED CARAMEL SURPRISE.

EASY PEASY PEANUT BRITTLE

Easy-peasy-orange-squeezy, this is an easy peanut brittle, perfect to keep in a jar on the side for teatime, or tied up with a bright orange ribbon for a Christmas gift. The sea salt gives it a delicious salted caramel flavour that will have everyone begging you to make another batch!

200g CASTER SUGAR
100g ROASTED PEANUTS
100g DARK TERRY'S CHOCOLATE ORANGE SEGMENTS, CHOPPED
1 tsp SEA SALT FLAKES

1. Line a baking tray with non-stick baking parchment.

2. Spread the sugar out in a frying pan and place over a medium heat for 5 minutes, or until it melts and starts to caramelize. Watch it carefully so it doesn't catch and burn and don't stir it – just tilt the pan occasionally so it spreads evenly.

3. When the sugar is amber in colour, stir in the peanuts and transfer to the lined baking tray, spreading it out thinly and evenly. Leave at room temperature until the brittle is completely cold and set hard (about half an hour).

4. Melt the Dark Terry's Chocolate Orange (see page 12).

5. Pour the melted chocolate over the top of the brittle to cover it completely. Sprinkle with the sea salt and set aside until the chocolate sets.

6. Break the peanut brittle into pieces and store in an airtight container for up to 2 weeks.

TRY THIS
THIS MOUTH-WATERING BRITTLE CAN ALSO BE MADE WITH WHITE TERRY'S CHOCOLATE ORANGE, OR WITH BLANCHED ALMONDS INSTEAD OF PEANUTS. YUM!

MAKES 50–60 SQUARES

PREP: 20 MINUTES
COOK: 15 MINUTES

FANCY FUDGE

Fudge, glorious fudge! Serve this mouth-watering delight as an after-dinner treat, or parcel it up in fancy wrapping and hand out as a tasty gift.

OIL, FOR GREASING
200g DARK TERRY'S CHOCOLATE ORANGE SEGMENTS
600g GRANULATED SUGAR
2 tbsp LIQUID GLUCOSE
600ml DOUBLE CREAM
200g BUTTER
2 tbsp ICING SUGAR, SIFTED

1. Lightly oil a 25 × 20cm cake tin or baking tray (one that has a 2cm raised edge) and line with baking parchment.

2. Melt the Dark Terry's Chocolate Orange (see page 12). Leave the bowl over the hot water to keep the chocolate soft.

3. Put the granulated sugar, glucose, cream and butter in a large heavy-based pan set over a low–medium heat. Stir until the sugar dissolves, then increase the heat and bring to the boil.

4. Reduce the heat immediately to medium and keep stirring for 5–10 minutes until the temperature on a sugar thermometer is 118°C (or just above soft ball stage – if you don't have a sugar thermometer, drop half a teaspoon of the mixture into a small bowl of cold water; if it's ready, it will form a small soft ball).

5. Remove from the heat and pour the liquid syrup into a food mixer. Beat on a low speed for 2–3 minutes, then whisk in the icing sugar. Add the melted chocolate and whisk until everything is well combined and smooth. Alternatively, beat in a bowl with a hand-held electric whisk.

6. Pour into the lined cake tin or baking tray, filling it to the top. Leave for several hours, or overnight, until completely cold and set. Cut into small squares and store in an airtight container for up to 2 weeks.

TIP: Keep stirring the fudge syrup all the time when it's heating up to soft ball stage. This will prevent it catching and sticking to the pan.

SMALLER BAKES

When you fancy something bigger than a bite but not quite as grand as a full dessert, Smaller Bakes are just the ticket. From blondies and brownies to cupcakes and éclairs, these are simple recipes that still produce fantabulous chocolate results, for an afternoon treat or a simple yet chocolatey evening pudding.

BLISSFUL BLONDIES

Just like their darker relative, the brownie, a blondie wants a glossy, crisp top and a gooey, oozy inside. And if you flavour them with orange zest and dip them into melted White Terry's Chocolate Orange, you'll soon see why blond(i)es have all the fun.

PREP: 20 MINUTES
COOK: 20–25 MINUTES

100g BUTTER
125g SOFT LIGHT BROWN
   SUGAR
2 MEDIUM FREE-RANGE
   EGGS
1 tsp VANILLA EXTRACT
GRATED ZEST OF 1 ORANGE
125g SELF-RAISING FLOUR,
   SIFTED
100g WHITE TERRY'S
   CHOCOLATE ORANGE
   SEGMENTS, ROUGHLY
   CHOPPED
SHREDDED COCONUT,
   FOR SPRINKLING

TRY THIS

THESE CAN BE MADE *EVEN*
RICHER BY FOLDING SOME
CHOPPED WHITE TERRY'S
CHOCOLATE ORANGE INTO
THE MIXTURE, OR ADDING
CHOPPED PECANS OR
WALNUTS IN BEFORE BAKING.

1. Preheat the oven to 190°C/170°C fan/gas mark 5. Lightly butter a 20cm square cake tin and line with baking parchment.

2. Melt the butter in a pan set over a low heat and then stir in the sugar. Increase the heat to medium; when it starts to colour and turn golden, remove from the heat.

3. Whisk the eggs, vanilla extract and orange zest in a large bowl and then beat in the butter and sugar mixture. Add the flour, folding it in gently with a metal spoon until everything is well combined and smooth. Transfer the mixture to the lined cake tin, spreading it out and smoothing the top.

4. Bake in the oven for 20–25 minutes until well risen and golden and a skewer inserted into the centre comes out clean. Leave the cake in the tin until it's completely cold and then cut into 12 squares.

5. Melt the White Terry's Chocolate Orange segments (see page 12).

6. Dip half of each blondie square into the melted chocolate and place on a baking sheet lined with baking parchment. Sprinkle with shredded coconut, pressing it lightly into the melted chocolate. Leave to cool at room temperature until the chocolate sets. Store the blondies in an airtight container for up to 3 days.

STRAWBERRY SUMMER BROWNIES

PREP: 15 MINUTES
COOK: 20 MINUTES
CHILL: 1 HOUR

A foolproof brownie recipe for a squidgy chocolate bake, with that classic hit of summer. Absolutely delicious for any picnic with friends, outside on a blanket or indoors under one!

1 MILK TERRY'S CHOCOLATE ORANGE
200g BUTTER
2 LARGE FREE-RANGE EGGS
130g CASTER SUGAR
½ tsp VANILLA EXTRACT
100g PLAIN FLOUR
50g UNSWEETENED COCOA POWDER
A PINCH OF SALT
400g LARGE STRAWBERRIES, HALVED

FOR THE TOPPING
300g DARK CHOCOLATE CHIPS
300g DOUBLE CREAM
16 MILK TERRY'S CHOCOLATE ORANGE SEGMENTS

1. Preheat the oven to 180°C/160°C fan/gas mark 4 and line a 20cm square cake tin with baking parchment.

2. Smash the Milk Chocolate Orange and place the segments into a pan. Add the butter and melt them together over a low–medium heat.

3. In a large bowl whisk together the eggs, sugar and vanilla extract, then stir in the melted butter and chocolate mixture.

4. In a medium bowl, combine the flour, cocoa powder and salt. Add the dry ingredients to the egg and chocolate mixture and stir until well combined.

5. Pour the mixture into the prepared cake tin and bake for 20 minutes. Once baked, leave to cool completely in the tin. Lay the halved strawberries evenly on top.

6. Prepare the topping: place the chocolate chips in a bowl, then heat the double cream over a medium heat until it just starts to simmer. Pour the cream over the chocolate chips and wait for 2 minutes before stirring constantly until the mixture is smooth. Pour this ganache over the strawberry layer.

7. Place the brownie in the fridge for 1 hour. Slice into squares and add a Chocolate Orange segment to the top of each one. Juicy, chocolatey and sweet – the only thing you have to do with these brownies is scoff and enjoy!

FANTASTIC FLAPJACKS

Calling all flapjack fanatics! These flapjacks take all the sweetness, nuttiness and crunchiness of your everyday flapjack, plus the goodness of oats, fruit and nuts, adding in chunky Terry's Chocolate Orange to nudge them from something special to *utterly* yummy.

250g GOLDEN SYRUP

250g UNSALTED BUTTER, PLUS EXTRA FOR GREASING

GRATED ZEST OF 1 ORANGE

300g JUMBO OATS

A PINCH OF SEA SALT

75g DRIED FRUIT, e.g. CRANBERRIES, CHERRIES, RAISINS

75g CHOPPED NUTS, e.g. PECANS, WALNUTS

100g MILK TERRY'S CHOCOLATE ORANGE SEGMENTS, CUT INTO SMALL CHUNKS

1. Preheat the oven to 180°C/160°C fan/gas mark 4. Butter a 20cm square cake tin and line it with baking parchment.

2. Put the golden syrup and butter into a pan and set over a medium heat. When the butter has melted into the syrup, stir in the orange zest, oats, sea salt, dried fruit, nuts and three-quarters of the chocolate.

3. Transfer to the lined tin, pressing the mixture into the corners, and smooth the top. Bake in the oven for 20 minutes until golden brown.

4. Sprinkle with the remaining chocolate chunks, pressing them in lightly, and set aside to cool. After 10 minutes, cut into 9 squares and leave until they are completely cold. The flapjacks will keep well stored in an airtight container for up to 5 days – if they haven't been eaten by then.

TRY THIS
IF YOU PREFER, YOU CAN USE WHITE OR DARK TERRY'S CHOCOLATE ORANGE, AND INSTEAD OF ADDING CHUNKS AT THE END, COVER THE FLAPJACKS WITH MELTED CHOCOLATE BEFORE LEAVING TO SET. NOW THAT'S A FLAPJACK.

MAKES
16

PREP: 20 MINUTES
COOK: 15–20 MINUTES

FINGER-LICKING CUPCAKES

Rich, moist and pretty as a picture, these cupcakes use the creaminess of Chocolate Orange to make a bake you won't forget. Top with your choice of Milk, Dark or White Terry's Chocolate Orange Buttercream for the final swirl of self-indulgence.

200g BUTTER, SOFTENED

200g CASTER SUGAR

2 MEDIUM FREE-RANGE EGGS

200g SELF-RAISING FLOUR

50g COCOA POWDER

GRATED ZEST OF 1 ORANGE

150g NATURAL LOW-FAT YOGHURT

1 QUANTITY TERRY'S CHOCOLATE ORANGE BUTTERCREAM (SEE PAGE 13)

TERRY'S CHOCOLATE ORANGE CRISPY ORANGES, TO DECORATE

YOU WILL NEED A PIPING BAG WITH A STAR-SHAPED NOZZLE

1. Preheat the oven to 180°C/160°C fan/gas mark 4. Place 16 paper muffin cases into 2 muffin tins.

2. Using a hand-held electric whisk or a food mixer, beat the butter and sugar together until light and fluffy. Beat in the eggs, one at a time, then sift in the flour and cocoa and mix in gently. Add the orange zest and yoghurt, mixing until smooth.

3. Divide the mixture between the paper cases and bake in the oven for 15–20 minutes until well risen and a thin skewer inserted into the centre of a cake comes out clean. Cool completely on a wire rack.

4. Spoon the buttercream into a piping bag fitted with a star nozzle and pipe large swirls on top of each cupcake, then decorate each with a Terry's Chocolate Orange Crispy Orange. Store the cakes in an airtight container for up to 3 days.

TRY THIS
WHY NOT TRY ADDING SOME GRATED ORANGE ZEST OR A DASH OF JUICE TO THE BUTTERCREAM? YOU CAN ALSO DECORATE THE BUTTERCREAM TOPPING WITH WHITE OR MILK TERRY'S CHOCOLATE ORANGE SEGMENTS FOR A TRULY DECADENT TREAT, OR AT EASTER, ADD SOME TERRY'S CHOCOLATE ORANGE MINI EGGS.

FLUTTERING BUTTERFLY CAKES

PREP: 20 MINUTES
COOK: 15–20 MINUTES

Suddenly your kitchen is full of people volunteering to help you cook. That's right – it's cupcake time! A cute snack, a treat at teatime, or a brilliant surprise in a lunchbox, these butterfly cakes will be flying out of there.

100g BUTTER

100g SOFT LIGHT BROWN SUGAR

2 MEDIUM FREE-RANGE EGGS, BEATEN

75g SELF-RAISING FLOUR, SIFTED

½ tsp BAKING POWDER

25g COCOA POWDER

GRATED ZEST OF 1 ORANGE

2 tbsp ORANGE JUICE

12 MILK TERRY'S CHOCOLATE ORANGE SEGMENTS

1. Preheat the oven to 180°C/160°C fan/gas mark 4. Place 12 paper cases in a 12-hole muffin tin.

2. In a food mixer, or using a hand-held electric whisk, beat the butter and sugar together until light and fluffy. Beat in the eggs, one at a time.

3. Sift the flour, baking powder and cocoa into the bowl and fold in gently. Lightly stir in the orange zest and loosen the mixture with the orange juice.

4. Divide the mixture between the paper cases and bake in the oven for 15–20 minutes until well risen and a thin skewer inserted into the centre of a cake comes out clean. Cool on a wire rack, then cut a shallow inverted cone piece out of the centre of each cake and set aside while you make the buttercream.

5. In a food mixer, or using a hand-held electric whisk, beat the butter with a little icing sugar until smooth. Sift in the rest of the icing sugar, a little at a time and beating well between each addition, until smooth and creamy.

FOR THE BUTTERCREAM

50g BUTTER, SOFTENED

100g ICING SUGAR, PLUS
  EXTRA FOR DUSTING

30g DARK TERRY'S
  CHOCOLATE ORANGE
  SEGMENTS

YOU WILL NEED A PIPING
BAG WITH A STAR-SHAPED
NOZZLE

6. Melt the Chocolate Orange segments (see page 12).

7. As soon as the chocolate starts to soften, add it to the buttercream and stir with a flat-bladed knife until it's thoroughly combined and evenly coloured. Work quickly to prevent the mixture separating.

8. Transfer to a piping bag fitted with a star-shaped nozzle and pipe a rosette into the dip on top of each cupcake. Cut each reserved cone in half to form 'wings' and place on top of the cakes.

9. Dust lightly with icing sugar and place a Terry's Chocolate Orange segment between each set of 'wings'. The cakes will keep well in an airtight container in a cool place for 3–4 days.

ELEGANT ÉCLAIRS

MAKES 12

PREP: 25 MINUTES
COOK: 35 MINUTES
CHILL: 30 MINUTES

A crowd-pleasing elegant favourite, these are actually much easier to make than you think. Make the choux pastry éclairs in advance and store them in an airtight container until you're ready to fill them, then coat with scrumptious Terry's Chocolate Orange glaze. Ooh la la! *See photo overleaf.*

FOR THE CHOUX PASTRY
240ml WATER
115g UNSALTED BUTTER
2 tbsp CASTER SUGAR
A PINCH OF SALT
115g PLAIN FLOUR, SIFTED
4 MEDIUM FREE-RANGE
  EGGS

FOR THE FILLING
300ml DOUBLE CREAM
1 tbsp ICING SUGAR
½ tsp VANILLA EXTRACT

1. Preheat the oven to 200°C/180°C fan/gas mark 6. Line a baking sheet with baking parchment.

2. Put the water, butter, sugar and salt in a pan and bring to the boil. Remove from the heat and tip in the flour. Beat vigorously with a wooden spoon until the mixture forms a ball that comes away from the sides of the pan.

3. Remove from the heat and beat in the eggs, one at a time and beating well between additions, until the choux pastry is glossy and smooth.

4. Spoon the mixture into a piping bag fitted with a 2cm round nozzle. Pipe 12 long strips, about 12cm long, on to the lined baking sheet.

5. Bake in the oven for 15 minutes, then reduce the heat to 170°C/150° fan/gas mark 3 and cook for a further 20 minutes, or until risen, crisp and golden brown. Remove and cool completely on a wire rack.

FOR THE TERRY'S CHOCOLATE ORANGE GLAZE

100g DARK TERRY'S CHOCOLATE ORANGE SEGMENTS, ROUGHLY CHOPPED

50g UNSALTED BUTTER, SOFTENED

YOU WILL NEED A PIPING BAG, A 2CM ROUND NOZZLE AND A MEDIUM STAR-SHAPED NOZZLE

6. Make the filling: whip the cream with the icing sugar and vanilla extract to stiff peaks. Transfer to a piping bag fitted with a medium star-shaped nozzle. Split the cold éclair shells in half lengthways and fill with the whipped cream, or make a small hole in each éclair and pipe the cream into the middle.

7. Make the glaze: melt the chocolate (see page 12). Add the butter and beat until smooth.

8. Coat the top half of each éclair with the glaze and chill in the fridge until it sets hard.

TRY THIS

ALREADY ONE OF THE BEST INDULGENCES AROUND, YOU CAN UP THE LUXURY FACTOR BY STIRRING SOME GRATED TERRY'S CHOCOLATE ORANGE, GRATED ORANGE ZEST OR CHOPPED STRAWBERRIES INTO THE WHIPPED CREAM. TASTY!

TIP: To check whether the éclair shells are cooked, tap them lightly on the base with your knuckles – they should sound hollow.

CHOCOLATE-SPECKLED GINGERBREAD LOAF

PREP: 15 MINUTES
COOK: 50 MINUTES

This light and chocolatey recipe is simple to make; but giving it 24 hours to rest once baked might be more than anyone can manage. It's worth the wait, though! Good luck . . .

60g BUTTER, PLUS EXTRA FOR GREASING
125g GOLDEN SYRUP
75g PLAIN FLOUR
25g SELF-RAISING FLOUR
25g COCOA POWDER
1 tsp BICARBONATE OF SODA
A PINCH OF SALT
2 tsp GROUND GINGER
1 tsp MIXED SPICE
100g SOFT LIGHT BROWN SUGAR
125ml MILK
1 MEDIUM FREE-RANGE EGG
GRATED ZEST AND JUICE OF 1 ORANGE
50g MILK OR DARK TERRY'S CHOCOLATE ORANGE SEGMENTS, CHOPPED

1. Preheat the oven to 170°C/150°C fan/gas mark 3. Butter a 900g loaf tin and line the base with baking parchment.

2. Stir the golden syrup and butter together in a pan set over a low heat until the butter melts.

3. Sift the flours, cocoa powder and bicarbonate of soda into a large bowl. Stir in the salt, spices and sugar.

4. Beat the milk and egg together and stir into the flour mixture, mixing well. Stir in the orange zest and juice and then add the melted butter and syrup, a little at a time, mixing between each addition. Stir in the chopped chocolate.

5. Transfer to the lined loaf tin and bake in the oven for 50 minutes, or until the cake is well risen and a skewer inserted into the middle comes out clean. Remove from the oven and leave in the tin for 10 minutes before turning out on to a wire rack.

6. When the cake is cold, wrap it in foil for 24 hours before serving cut into slices. It is deliciously moist and will keep well for up to 3 days.

TRY THIS
TO TURN THIS FROM A TEATIME TREAT INTO A SPECIAL DESSERT, ADD CHOPPED STEM GINGER TO THE CAKE MIXTURE AND POUR MELTED MILK, DARK OR WHITE TERRY'S CHOCOLATE ORANGE OVER THE COOLED CAKE IN DELICIOUS SWIRLS AND DRIZZLES BEFORE SERVING. WHO COULD SAY NO?

MARVELLOUS MERINGUES

Simple to make, stunning to look at , delicious to eat! Although you can beat the eggs and sugar by hand, it's much quicker and easier to use a food mixer or hand-held electric whisk. Whatever your method, these little puffs of sweetness are worth it.

PREP: 15 MINUTES
COOK: 2 HOURS

4 MEDIUM FREE-RANGE EGG WHITES

A PINCH OF SALT

225g CASTER SUGAR

75g DARK TERRY'S CHOCOLATE ORANGE SEGMENTS

300ml DOUBLE CREAM

GRATED ZEST OF 1 ORANGE

2 KNOBS OF STEM GINGER IN SYRUP, FINELY DICED

TRY THIS

THESE ALSO LOOK GORGEOUS DUSTED WITH A LITTLE CINNAMON, OR, INSTEAD OF COATING WITH MELTED CHOCOLATE, ADD FINELY CHOPPED CHOCOLATE TO THE WHIPPED CREAM. EITHER WAY, EVERYONE WILL COME BACK FOR MORE.

1. Preheat the oven to 110°C/90°C fan/gas mark ½. Line 2 baking trays with baking parchment.

2. Using a food mixer or a hand-held electric whisk, beat the egg whites and salt until they form stiff peaks. Adds 3 tablespoons of the sugar and beat again until stiff and glossy. Fold in the rest of the sugar in a figure-of-eight motion with a metal spoon.

3. Using a dessertspoon, drop spoonfuls of the mixture on to the lined baking trays, leaving plenty of space around them. You should end up with 12 meringues.

4. Bake in the oven for 2 hours, or until the meringues are dry. Peel them off the paper and leave on a wire rack until completely cold.

5. Melt the Terry's Chocolate Orange segments (see page 12).

6. Dip the flat side of each meringue into the melted chocolate – just enough to coat it lightly – and leave, chocolate-side up, until set hard.

7. Whip the cream until it stands in soft peaks. Stir in the orange zest and stem ginger and use to sandwich the meringues together in pairs. Serve immediately.

CELEBRATION CAKES

If ever there was an ingredient that was just meant for celebration, it's the Terry's Chocolate Orange – and what better way to use it than in (and on) a cake. Bake one for a birthday, for Christmas, to congratulate a loved one or just because it's a Tuesday. Just make sure someone saves you a slice . . .

SERVES
8

PREP: 25 MINUTES
COOK: 45 MINUTES

CARROT CAKE

Oh, carrot cake! A perfect mixture of spice and sweet, this cake is complemented by the creamy Terry's Chocolate Orange icing (almost enough to make the cake blush).

175g SOFT LIGHT BROWN SUGAR

120ml SUNFLOWER OIL

3 MEDIUM FREE-RANGE EGGS, BEATEN

225g CARROTS, GRATED

GRATED ZEST AND JUICE OF 1 ORANGE

175g WHOLEMEAL SELF-RAISING FLOUR

1 tsp BAKING POWDER

1 tsp GROUND CINNAMON

½ tsp GRATED NUTMEG

WHITE OR MILK TERRY'S CHOCOLATE ORANGE SEGMENTS, TO DECORATE

FOR THE ICING

180g WHITE TERRY'S CHOCOLATE ORANGE SEGMENTS

100g UNSALTED BUTTER, SOFTENED

30g ICING SUGAR

GRATED ZEST OF 1 ORANGE

1. Preheat the oven to 180°C/160°C fan/gas mark 4. Lightly oil a 20cm round cake tin and line with baking parchment.

2. In a food mixer or food processor, beat the sugar, oil and eggs until well blended. (Alternatively, use a hand-held electric whisk.) Beat in the grated carrots and orange zest and juice. Sift in the flour, baking powder and spices and mix thoroughly.

3. Pour the cake mixture into the lined cake tin and smooth the top. Bake in the oven for 45 minutes, or until well risen and a skewer inserted into the centre comes out clean. Leave the cake to cool in the tin.

4. Make the icing: melt the White Terry's Chocolate Orange segments (see page 12). Set aside.

5. Use a hand-held electric whisk to beat the butter and icing sugar together until fluffy. Add the orange zest and melted chocolate and beat until smooth.

6. Spread the icing over the top and sides of the cake and decorate with Chocolate Orange segments. Keep in a sealed container in the fridge for 3–4 days.

TRY THIS

FOR A BIT OF A CHANGE, ADD SOME SHREDDED COCONUT TO THE CAKE MIXTURE OR SPRINKLE SOME OVER THE FROSTING, ADD A SPLASH OF GRAND MARNIER TO THE ICING OR STIR IN SOME CHOPPED OR GRATED TERRY'S CHOCOLATE ORANGE TO THE CAKE MIXTURE BEFORE BAKING. TOO GOOD FOR RABBITS!

HIDDEN TREASURE MINI EGGS PIÑATA CAKE

PREP: 45 MINUTES
COOK: 20 MINUTES
CHILL: 1 HOUR

A big occasion needs a big cake, and this is the perfect recipe – delicious, playful and truly, truly scrumptious. Let's get this party started!
See photo overleaf.

FOR THE CAKE

200ml MILK, AT ROOM TEMPERATURE
1 tsp LEMON JUICE
85g UNSWEETENED COCOA POWDER
260g PLAIN FLOUR
320g CASTER SUGAR
1 tbsp BAKING POWDER
1 tbsp BICARBONATE OF SODA
A PINCH OF SALT
3 LARGE FREE-RANGE EGGS
70ml NEUTRAL OIL
1 tsp VANILLA EXTRACT
100ml HOT WATER

1. Preheat the oven to 180°C/160°C fan/gas mark 4. Grease 3 x 20cm round cake tins and line the base of each one with baking parchment.

2. Stir together the milk and lemon juice and set aside. Put the cocoa powder, flour, sugar, baking powder, bicarbonate of soda and salt into a large bowl and mix to combine.

3. Beat the eggs in a separate bowl and then stir in the oil, milk and lemon juice mixture, vanilla extract and hot water.

4. Pour the wet ingredients into the dry and mix until well combined. Divide the mixture evenly between the 3 tins and bake for 20 minutes, or until a toothpick inserted in the centre of the cakes comes out clean. Leave to cool in the tins for 10 minutes before transferring to wire racks to cool completely.

5. For the frosting, melt three-quarters of the Terry's Chocolate Orange (see page 12). Set aside.

6. Whip the double cream until stiff peaks start to form, then add the mascarpone and whip again. Fold in the melted chocolate, then cover and chill for 1 hour.

FOR THE FROSTING AND DECORATION

1 MILK TERRY'S CHOCOLATE ORANGE, BROKEN INTO SEGMENTS, PLUS EXTRA FOR DECORATING

300ml DOUBLE CREAM,

250g MASCARPONE

2 PACKS TERRY'S CHOCOLATE ORANGE MINI EGGS

7. Using an 8cm cookie cutter, cut out a circle from the centre of one of the cakes. (Crumble this up and set aside for later – it's important!)

8. Build your cake, starting with a whole layer. Spread some of the chocolate frosting around (avoiding the centre) and top with the cut-out cake. Fill the centre with most of the Terry's Chocolate Orange Mini Eggs and spread the frosting around the edge before topping with the final layer.

9. Frost the top and sides of the cake and decorate with the remaining frosting. Decorate the top with the crumbled cake, remaining Mini Eggs and Chocolate Orange segments. Now watch your guests line up to enjoy the piñata surprise as well as the delicious cake. Fiesta!

TRIUMPHANT TRUFFLE CAKE

Decadent, rich and impressive, this special-occasion cake will thrill chocoholics. Make the cake a couple of days beforehand, then fill and ice on the day you serve it up for your eager crowd.

150g BUTTER, SOFTENED, PLUS EXTRA FOR GREASING

200g GOLDEN CASTER SUGAR

3 MEDIUM FREE-RANGE EGGS

150g SELF-RAISING FLOUR

1 tsp BAKING POWDER

50g COCOA POWDER

GRATED ZEST AND JUICE OF 1 ORANGE

4 tbsp APRICOT JAM, FOR BRUSHING

½ QUANTITY TERRY'S CHOCOLATE ORANGE BUTTERCREAM (SEE PAGE 13)

TERRY'S CHOCOLATE ORANGE TRUFFLES, TO DECORATE

1. Preheat the oven to 180°C/160°C fan/gas mark 4. Lightly grease 2 × 20cm round cake tins with butter and line the bases with baking parchment.

2. In a food mixer, or using a hand-held electric whisk, beat the butter and sugar until creamy, pale and fluffy. Beat in the eggs, one at a time and adding a little of the flour with them and beating in between. Sift in the remaining flour, baking powder and cocoa powder and beat into the mixture with the orange zest. The mixture will be quite stiff, so loosen it with the orange juice.

3. Transfer the mixture to the lined cake tins and bake in the oven for 25–30 minutes, or until the sponges are well risen and a skewer inserted into the middle comes out clean.

4. Heat the jam in a small pan set over a low heat. Stir and brush gently over the warm sponges. Leave in the tins for 10 minutes, then turn out on to a wire rack to cool while you make the truffle icing.

FOR THE TRUFFLE ICING

1 DARK TERRY'S CHOCOLATE ORANGE, BROKEN INTO SEGMENTS

50g UNSALTED BUTTER, DICED

3 tbsp DOUBLE CREAM

5. Melt the Dark Terry's Chocolate Orange segments with the butter (see page 12). Set aside for 10 minutes to cool, then stir in the cream.

6. Sandwich the sponges together with the buttercream and place the cake on a wire rack with a plate underneath. Spread the truffle icing over the top and sides of the cake to cover it, smoothing it out with a palette knife. Decorate the top with the Terry's Chocolate Orange Truffles and chill in the fridge until firm. The cake will keep well in the fridge for 2–3 days.

TRY THIS

TO UP THE LUSCIOUS ORANGE FLAVOURS, TOP THE CAKE WITH CANDIED ORANGE PEEL AND MILK TERRY'S CHOCOLATE ORANGE SEGMENTS, AND INSTEAD OF ORANGE JUICE IN THE SPONGE, TRY A LITTLE GRAND MARNIER TO FLAVOUR IT. ORANGE YOU GLAD YOU TRIED IT?

DAZZLING DRIZZLE CAKE

SERVES 8

PREP: 20 MINUTES
COOK: 45–50 MINUTES

Baking can sometimes seem tricky, but this is an easy and tasty cake to get you going. The orange syrup and ground almonds help keep it moist and flavourful, so just relax, serve up and enjoy.

225g BUTTER, SOFTENED
225g CASTER SUGAR
4 MEDIUM FREE-RANGE EGGS
175g SELF-RAISING FLOUR
50g GROUND ALMONDS
GRATED ZEST AND JUICE OF 1 ORANGE
100g MILK OR DARK TERRY'S CHOCOLATE ORANGE SEGMENTS, CHOPPED

FOR THE ORANGE SYRUP
JUICE OF 1 ORANGE
4 tbsp CASTER SUGAR

1. Preheat the oven to 180°C/160°C fan/gas mark 4. Butter a 900g loaf tin and line with baking parchment.

2. Beat the butter and sugar together in a food mixer, or using a hand-held electric whisk, until creamy, pale and fluffy.

3. Beat in the eggs, one at a time, adding a little of the flour with them and beating between each addition. Sift in the remaining flour and beat into the mixture with the ground almonds. Stir in the grated orange zest and juice, then gently fold in the chocolate, distributing it evenly throughout the mixture. If it seems too thick, you can loosen it gradually with 1–2 tablespoons of milk.

4. Transfer to the lined loaf tin and smooth the top. Bake in the oven for 45–50 minutes, or until well risen and golden brown. Test whether the cake is cooked by inserting a skewer into the centre – it should come out clean. Set aside to cool in the tin while you make the syrup.

5. Heat the orange juice and sugar in a small pan set over a low heat, stirring until the sugar dissolves. Pierce the top of the cake several times with a skewer and pour over the warm syrup. Leave the cake to cool in the tin and absorb all the syrup before turning it out and removing the paper wrapping.

WONDERFULLY WHITE CHOCOLATE CAKE

SERVES 8

PREP: 20 MINUTES
COOK: 30 MINUTES
CHILL: 1 HOUR

Stunning and fun, this cake is enjoyable year-round — serve at Christmas, with snowmen and reindeer frolicking in the snow, or at Easter, piled high with White Terry's Chocolate Orange Mini Eggs. Or at any time, just because you fancy it!

175g BUTTER, SOFTENED, PLUS EXTRA FOR GREASING

175g CASTER SUGAR

4 MEDIUM FREE-RANGE EGGS

100g SELF-RAISING FLOUR

1 tsp BAKING POWDER

100g GROUND ALMONDS

A FEW DROPS OF VANILLA EXTRACT

GRATED ZEST OF 3 ORANGES

JUICE OF 1 ORANGE

GRATED WHITE AND MILK TERRY'S CHOCOLATE ORANGE SEGMENTS, TO DECORATE

1. Preheat the oven to 180°C/160°C fan/gas mark 4. Lightly grease 2 × 20cm round cake tins with butter and line the bases with baking parchment.

2. In a food mixer, or with a hand-held electric whisk, beat the butter and sugar until creamy, pale and fluffy.

3. Beat in the eggs, one at a time and adding a little of the flour with them and beating in between. Sift in the remaining flour and the baking powder and beat into the mixture with the ground almonds, vanilla extract and orange zest. The mixture will be quite stiff, so loosen it a little with the orange juice.

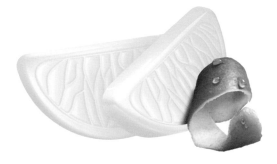

68

FOR THE WHITE
TERRY'S CHOCOLATE
ORANGE FROSTING
1 WHITE TERRY'S
  CHOCOLATE ORANGE
150ml CRÈME FRAÎCHE

4. Transfer the mixture to the lined cake tins and bake in the oven for 30 minutes, or until the sponges are well risen, golden and spring back when pressed lightly with a finger.

5. Leave to cool in the tins for 10 minutes, then invert the sponges on to a wire rack, peel off the baking parchment and leave until cold.

6. To make the frosting, melt the White Terry's Chocolate Orange segments (see page 12). Remove from the heat. Meanwhile, whip the crème fraîche in a bowl until it thickens and forms soft peaks. Gently stir in the melted chocolate until well blended and smooth.

7. Spread half of the frosting over one of the sponges and place the other sponge on top. Top with the remaining frosting and chill in the fridge until set. This will take at least 1 hour. Before serving, sprinkle the grated chocolate over the top and then cut into slices.

TRY THIS
YOU CAN DECORATE THIS HOWEVER YOU LIKE – WITH CHOCOLATE CURLS, WHITE TERRY'S CHOCOLATE ORANGE SEGMENTS OR WITH SPRINKLES OF SHREDDED COCONUT. YOU COULD ALSO SWAP THE WHITE TERRY'S CHOCOLATE ORANGE SEGMENTS FOR MILK OR DARK – THE ONLY LIMIT IS YOUR IMAGINATION! (AND HOW MUCH WEIGHT THE CAKE WILL HOLD.)

TRIPLE CHOCOLATE CHRISTMAS TREE CAKE

SERVES 8–10

PREP: 40 MINUTES
COOK: 35 MINUTES
FREEZE: 1 HOUR

If you ever wanted a show-stopper of a cake with only a casual afternoon's effort, this Christmas tree cake with three different types of Terry's Chocolate Orange in it is just what you've been looking for. Perfect for a festive party or a cosy December teatime. *See photo overleaf.*

---

1 MILK TERRY'S CHOCOLATE ORANGE

90g BUTTER

3 MEDIUM FREE-RANGE EGGS, SEPARATED

150g SOFT DARK BROWN SUGAR

150ml MILK

215g PLAIN FLOUR

2 tsp BAKING POWDER

3 tbsp UNSWEETENED COCOA POWDER

1 tsp VANILLA EXTRACT

40g CASTER SUGAR

1. Start by making the chocolate Christmas trees for the decoration. Melt the Dark Terry's Chocolate Orange segments (see page 12), then let the chocolate cool down. Once it's cool but still soft, spoon into a piping bag. Line a baking tray with parchment paper, draw five trees with the piping bag and place the tray in the fridge.

2. While the chocolate sets, make the cake sponge. Preheat the oven to 180°C/160°C fan/gas mark 4 and line a 20cm round cake tin with baking parchment. Smash the Terry's Milk Chocolate Orange into segments and add to a pan with the butter. Melt together over a low–medium heat.

3. Put the egg yolks and soft dark brown sugar into a bowl and stir until combined. Add the milk, flour, baking powder, cocoa powder and vanilla extract, along with the melted chocolate and butter mixture. Whisk together until completely combined.

4. Put the egg whites into a clean bowl and beat with a hand-held electric whisk until soft peaks form. Gradually add the caster sugar, then use a spatula to gently fold the whisked egg whites into the chocolate mixture, a third at a time. Pour the mixture into the prepared cake tin and bake for 35 minutes. Set aside

300ml DOUBLE CREAM
1 VANILLA POD
1 WHITE TERRY'S
   CHOCOLATE ORANGE,
   SEGMENTS CHOPPED
30g BUTTER

FOR THE DECORATION
ICING SUGAR, FOR DUSTING
1 DARK TERRY'S CHOCOLATE
   ORANGE, BROKEN INTO
   SEGMENTS

YOU WILL NEED A PIPING
BAG WITH A SMALL
ROUND NOZZLE

to cool for 10 minutes before transferring the cake to a wire rack to cool completely while you make the white chocolate ganache.

5. Pour the double cream into a pan and scrape the seeds from the vanilla pod into it. Put the chopped White Terry's Chocolate Orange segments into a bowl. Bring the cream to a simmer, then remove from heat and pour a third of the hot cream over the chopped chocolate and stir. Repeat with the remaining cream until the chocolate is completely melted. Add the butter and stir well. Place a sheet of cling film directly on top of the mixture and set aside in the freezer for 1 hour. Remove and whisk for a few minutes to get a firm ganache.

6. To finish, spread the creamy white ganache on top of the cake, then dress with the chocolate trees and some icing sugar. Decorate with a few Dark Terry's Chocolate Orange segments.

TRY THIS
IF YOU'VE GOT ANY MINIATURE CHRISTMAS DECORATIONS IN THE HOUSE, WHY NOT ADD A REINDEER, ROBIN OR A TINY PILE OF PRESENTS TO THE WINTER FOREST?

YOU'LL WANT MORE YULE LOG

PREP: 20 MINUTES
COOK: 15–20 MINUTES

This mouth-watering festive yule log is not just a simple Swiss roll; it's a rich and special treat for after a meal, or as a dessert at Christmas. Just pile it high with robins and holly, slice up and make merry.

OIL, FOR BRUSHING

175g DARK TERRY'S CHOCOLATE ORANGE SEGMENTS

2 tbsp HOT WATER

5 MEDIUM FREE-RANGE EGGS, SEPARATED

175g CASTER SUGAR

ICING SUGAR, FOR DUSTING

300ml DOUBLE CREAM

GRATED ZEST OF 1 ORANGE

1. Preheat the oven to 180°C/160°C fan/gas mark 4. Lightly brush a 34 × 23cm Swiss roll tin with oil and line with baking parchment so it comes up the sides of the tin.

2. Melt the Dark Terry's Chocolate Orange segments (see page 12). Add the hot water and stir gently.

3. Put the egg yolks and sugar into a bowl and use a hand-held electric whisk to beat them together until pale, thick and creamy. Stir in the melted chocolate until well blended.

4. In a clean, dry bowl, beat the egg whites until they form stiff peaks. Stir a spoonful of egg white into the chocolate mixture to loosen it and then gently fold in the remainder in a figure-of-eight motion with a metal spoon.

5. Transfer to the lined tin and level the top with a palette knife. Bake in the oven for 15–20 minutes, or until risen, springy and firm on top. Carefully slide the sponge, still on its baking parchment, out of the tin and on to a wire rack. Cover with a clean tea towel dampened with water and leave until cold.

6. When you're ready to assemble the yule log, place a large sheet of baking parchment on a work surface and sift some icing sugar over it. Place the cold sponge, baking parchment side up, on top of the icing sugar, and then carefully peel off the paper.

7. Beat the cream in a food mixer, or use a hand-held electric whisk, until it holds its shape. Take care not to overbeat it – it shouldn't be really stiff. Stir in the orange zest and spread evenly over the sponge, leaving a border of 1cm around the edges.

8. Using the paper to help you, roll up the sponge like a Swiss roll from one short end. It may well crack a little but don't worry about that. Transfer to a serving plate with the join underneath, then dust with icing sugar and decorate, if wished, with holly or Christmas cake decorations. The Yule Log will keep well in an airtight container in the fridge for 2 days.

DESSERTS

At the end of a perfect meal, what could be better than a perfect Terry's Chocolate Orange dessert? Profiteroles, tiramisu, tarts, ice creams and – of course – chocolate mousse. With serving suggestions and variations for each recipe, there's something here for every table, from light and creamy to wickedly chocolatey and indulgent.

FABULOUS FONDUE

PREP: 10 MINUTES
COOK: 5 MINUTES

This fudgy chocolate fondue makes a delicious but casual dessert for parties, even if you might get the occasional drip of chocolate on your table. When it's this tasty, who cares about the drips?

300ml DOUBLE CREAM
200g DARK TERRY'S CHOCOLATE ORANGE SEGMENTS, CHOPPED
1½ tbsp GOLDEN SYRUP
25g UNSALTED BUTTER, DICED

FOR DIPPING
MARSHMALLOWS
CUBED BANANA, MANGO, PINEAPPLE, PEAR, STRAWBERRIES
ORANGE AND MANDARIN SEGMENTS
CHOCOLATE WAFERS AND WAFER STICKS

YOU WILL NEED SHORT BAMBOO OR WOODEN SKEWERS

1. Put the cream into a pan and set over a low heat. When it's hot, remove from the heat and add the chocolate. Stir gently until it starts to melt into the cream.

2. Stir in the golden syrup and butter until the butter melts, then continue to stir gently until the sauce is smooth and glossy.

3. Leave in the pan or transfer to a serving bowl. Serve immediately with a selection of dippers. Let everyone dip in and help themselves. So it might get a little chocolatey, but who's going to mind?

TRY THIS
IF YOU'VE GOT A LARGE CROWD OVER, WHY NOT MAKE A BOWL EACH OF WHITE, MILK AND DARK TERRY'S CHOCOLATE ORANGE DIPPING FONDUE?

LUXURY PROFITEROLES

Profiteroles – the mouth-sized pastry delights of the entertaining world. You'll quickly discover how easy they are, and once your guests taste these Chocolate Orange versions they'll be requested again and again.

FOR THE CHOUX PASTRY

85g BUTTER, CUBED
200ml WATER
100g PLAIN FLOUR, SIFTED
A PINCH OF SALT
3 MEDIUM FREE-RANGE
   EGGS

FOR THE FILLING AND SAUCE

300ml DOUBLE CREAM
1 tbsp ICING SUGAR, SIFTED
1 QUANTITY DARK TERRY'S
   CHOCOLATE ORANGE
   SAUCE (SEE PAGE 16)

YOU WILL NEED A PIPING
BAG WITH A SMALL NOZZLE

1. Preheat the oven to 200°C/180°C fan/gas mark 6. Line a baking sheet with baking parchment.

2. Put the butter and water in a pan and set over a medium heat. When the butter melts, increase the heat and bring to the boil.

3. Add the flour and salt and immediately take the pan off the heat. Beat until the mixture is thick and smooth and forms a ball that comes away from the sides of the pan. Set aside to cool for 5 minutes and then beat in the eggs, one at a time, beating well between additions, until the choux pastry is glossy and smooth.

4. Drop tablespoonfuls of the mixture on to the lined baking sheet, leaving plenty of space around each one. Bake in the oven for 20–25 minutes until well risen, puffy and golden brown. Transfer to a wire rack and leave to cool completely.

5. Use a hand-held electric whisk to whip the cream for the filling until it stands in stiff peaks, then beat in the icing sugar. Use to fill a piping bag fitted with a small nozzle, then make a hole in each profiterole with a skewer and pipe in the cream.

6. Make the Dark Terry's Chocolate Orange Sauce. Divide the profiteroles between 4 serving bowls and spoon the sauce over the top.

PREP: 15 MINUTES

UNFORGETTABLE AFFOGATO

Transporting you to the bustling bars of Italy, this dessert is so quick and easy, you won't make it just once. If you don't have any Chocolate Orange Ice Cream, just use a good-quality vanilla, chocolate or coffee one instead, close your eyes and taste the pleasure. *Prego*!

240ml FRESHLY MADE STRONG ESPRESSO COFFEE (4 LONG SHOTS)

4 SCOOPS OF TERRY'S CHOCOLATE ORANGE ICE CREAM (SEE PAGE 94)

60g DARK TERRY'S CHOCOLATE ORANGE SEGMENTS, CHOPPED

1. Chill 4 small glasses or coffee cups.

2. Make the coffee in an espresso machine or a stovetop mocha pot. It must be piping hot.

3. Using a 50g ice-cream scoop, put a scoop of ice cream in each chilled glass or cup. Pour over the hot espresso and sprinkle with the chopped chocolate.

4. Serve immediately while the ice cream is still cold and starting to melt and the espresso is hot.

TRY THIS
SPRINKLE WITH SOME CHOPPED WHITE TERRY'S CHOCOLATE ORANGE FOR A LITTLE SOMETHING EXTRA, AND IMAGINE YOURSELF IN ROME.

PREP: 20 MINUTES
COOK: 5 MINUTES
CHILL: 3+ HOURS

SOOTHING PANNA COTTA

In Italian, *panna cotta* literally means 'cooked cream', which can be quite a delicate dessert. But the addition of Chocolate Orange lifts it into something much richer and more special — and the wonderful wobble is just a bonus.

---

1 VANILLA POD
2½ tsp POWDERED GELATINE
GRATED ZEST OF 1 ORANGE
300ml DOUBLE CREAM
300ml MILK
6 tbsp CASTER SUGAR
50g DARK TERRY'S CHOCOLATE ORANGE SEGMENTS, GRATED
30g DARK TERRY'S CHOCOLATE ORANGE SEGMENTS
STRAWBERRIES AND RASPBERRIES, TO SERVE

1. Use a sharp knife to cut open the vanilla pod from end to end and scrape out the seeds. Set aside.

2. Put 2 tablespoons of cold water in a pan and sprinkle the gelatine over the top. Leave for 5 minutes until spongy and then set over a low heat for 5 minutes, stirring occasionally until the gelatine dissolves. Do not allow it to boil.

3. Place the vanilla pod and seeds in a second pan with the orange zest, cream, milk, sugar and grated chocolate. Set over a low heat and simmer gently for 5 minutes, stirring occasionally to dissolve the sugar and melt the chocolate.

4. Remove the vanilla pod and stir in the dissolved gelatine.

5. Divide the mixture between 6 ramekins or small glasses, then cover and chill in the fridge for at least 3 hours, or until the panna cotta sets. Don't worry if it's not super-firm – it should be a soft set with the slightest hint of a wobble.

6. Shortly before serving, melt the remaining segments (see page 12). Leave for 5 minutes to cool slightly.

7. Drizzle the melted chocolate in a backward-and-forward zigzag pattern over the panna cottas so it sets in streaks. Chill in the fridge until set and serve with extra segments and fresh strawberries or raspberries.

TEMPTING ORANGE-Y TIRAMISU

Creamy and rich, this wonderful dessert doesn't need a special occasion to be shared, and the melted Chocolate Orange lifts it into a whole new glorious dimension. Make this the day before to let the flavours really develop in the cool of the fridge.

PREP: 15 MINUTES
CHILL: 4+ HOURS

1 MEDIUM FREE-RANGE EGG YOLK

2 tbsp CASTER SUGAR

250g MASCARPONE

250ml DOUBLE CREAM

60g DARK TERRY'S CHOCOLATE ORANGE SEGMENTS

175ml HOT STRONG BLACK COFFEE, e.g. ESPRESSO

1 tbsp ORANGE OR COFFEE LIQUEUR

200g ITALIAN SAVOIARDI SPONGE FINGERS

GRATED DARK TERRY'S CHOCOLATE ORANGE, FOR SPRINKLING

1. Beat the egg yolk and sugar together in a bowl. Whisk in the mascarpone, a little at a time, until smooth and thoroughly blended. Add the cream and whisk well until stiff. Use a food mixer or a hand-held electric whisk, if wished.

2. Melt the Chocolate Orange segments (see page 12), then beat the chocolate into the creamy mascarpone mixture.

3. Pour the hot coffee into another bowl and stir in the liqueur. Dip some sponge fingers into the hot coffee, just long enough that they absorb the liquid but keep their shape. Arrange a layer of them in a large, shallow serving dish.

4. Cover with a layer of chocolate mascarpone, smoothing it gently over the top. Repeat with another layer of soaked sponge fingers and chocolate mascarpone, alternating the layers until everything is used up and finishing with a layer of chocolate mascarpone.

5. Sprinkle the grated chocolate over the top and chill in the fridge for at least 4 hours before serving.

TRY THIS

AMARETTI BISCUITS ARE ALSO DELICIOUS, IN PLACE OF THE SPONGE FINGER BISCUITS. YOU CAN ALSO DUST THE TOP OF THE DESSERT WITH SOME COCOA POWDER FOR A FINAL TOUCH. WARNING: THERE WON'T BE ANY LEFTOVERS . . .

PERFECT POACHED PEARS

Just the thing for a cool autumn day, this wonderful dessert celebrates the marriage made in heaven that is pear and chocolate. Consider yourself invited to make the most of that delicious union.

750ml WHITE WINE OR WATER

1 CINNAMON STICK

2 CLOVES

1 VANILLA POD

1 ORANGE, HALVED

125g SUGAR

4 SLIGHTLY UNDERRIPE PEARS, e.g. COMICE OR WILLIAMS

1 QUANTITY DARK TERRY'S CHOCOLATE ORANGE SAUCE (SEE PAGE 16)

TRY THIS

WHY NOT USE A LEMON INSTEAD OF AN ORANGE IN THE POACHING LIQUID, OR SUBSTITUTE RED WINE FOR WHITE? SERVE WITH WHIPPED CREAM DUSTED WITH GROUND CINNAMON.

1. Preheat the oven to 200°C/180°C fan/gas mark 6.

2. Put the wine or water, spices, vanilla pod, orange halves and sugar in a pan. Set over a medium heat, stirring until the sugar dissolves, then turn up the heat and bring to the boil. Remove from the heat.

3. Peel the pears and remove the cores with an apple corer or sharp knife (leave the stalks intact). Place the pears in an ovenproof dish (not too large – just big enough for them to fit on their sides). Pour the poaching liquid over the top, tucking the spices and orange halves around them.

4. Cover and poach in the oven for 40–45 minutes, turning them halfway. To test if they're cooked, pierce with a skewer or the point of a sharp knife. They should be tender but still hold their shape.

5. While the pears are cooking, make the Dark Chocolate Orange Sauce.

6. Remove the pears from the poaching liquid and stand them upright in 4 dishes. Spoon or drizzle the hot sauce over the top.

7. Alternatively, transfer the poaching liquid (having removed the orange halves, spices and vanilla pod) to a pan and set over a low–medium heat. Simmer until it reduces by half to a syrup. Pour over the pears and serve warm or chilled with the chocolate sauce.

BREAD & BUTTER & CHOCOLATE ORANGE PUDDING

PREP: 15 MINUTES
SOAK: 10–15 MINUTES
COOK: 35–40 MINUTES

Comfort food at its best is like a warm hug, just what you need on a cold winter's day. Adding Terry's Chocolate Orange to the creamy custard in this pudding turns the comfort into true love.

40g BUTTER, SOFTENED, PLUS EXTRA FOR GREASING

6 MEDIUM SLICES OF WHITE BREAD

75g RAISINS OR SULTANAS

3 MEDIUM FREE-RANGE EGGS

50g CASTER SUGAR

450ml MILK (OR USE HALF MILK AND HALF CREAM)

GRATED ZEST OF 1 ORANGE

75g DARK TERRY'S CHOCOLATE ORANGE SEGMENTS

1. Lightly butter a 1 litre baking dish.

2. Butter the bread and cut each slice into triangles. Arrange them, buttered side up and overlapping, in the baking dish. Scatter the raisins or sultanas between them and over the top.

3. In a bowl, beat the eggs and sugar together until well blended. Put the milk or milk and cream with the orange zest in a pan and bring to the boil. Pour it over the egg and sugar mixture, stirring until smooth and custard-like.

4. Melt the Terry's Chocolate Orange segments (see page 12), then mix into the custard. Pour over the bread and leave to soak for 10–15 minutes before baking. Preheat the oven to 180°C/160°C fan/gas mark 4.

5. Bake in the oven for 35–40 minutes, or until the chocolate custard is set but still a little bit wobbly. Serve hot with cream, crème fraîche or ice cream.

TRY THIS
FOR A TOUCH OF LUXURY, USE SLICED BRIOCHE OR PANETTONE INSTEAD OF BREAD, AND DRIZZLE MELTED CHOCOLATE ACROSS THE BAKED PUDDING. WHO KNEW HUGS WERE BETTER WHEN YOU ADDED CHOCOLATE?

PREP: 20 MINUTES
CHILL: 4 HOURS

VELVETY WHITE CHOCOLATE ORANGE MOUSSE

Pretty and sweet, these little chocolate mousses can be made earlier in the day or the night before and chilled in the fridge. Jazz them up with raspberries or serve them with strawberries and little mint leaves on the side for a summery touch.

180ml DOUBLE CREAM

2 MEDIUM FREE-RANGE EGG WHITES

180g WHITE TERRY'S CHOCOLATE ORANGE SEGMENTS

70ml MILK

GRATED WHITE OR MILK TERRY'S CHOCOLATE ORANGE, FOR SPRINKLING

1. Use a hand-held electric whisk to whip the cream until it forms soft peaks. In another clean, dry bowl, whisk the egg whites until they are stiff.

2. Melt the Chocolate Orange segments (see page 12).

3. Warm the milk in a pan set over a medium heat, then stir it into the melted chocolate with a flat-bladed knife. Gently fold in the whipped cream until evenly coloured and then fold in the egg whites in the same way, taking care not to overmix.

4. Divide the mixture between 4 ramekins, pots or small serving dishes and chill in the fridge for 4 hours, or until set. Serve sprinkled with grated chocolate.

TRY THIS
THERE'S ALWAYS THE OPTION TO SWITCH THE CHOCOLATE FOR MILK OR DARK CHOCOLATE ORANGE INSTEAD — AND WHY NOT TRY INFUSING THE WARMED MILK WITH SOME VANILLA EXTRACT, A STRIP OF ORANGE RIND OR SOME CARDAMOM PODS?

**SERVES
4–6**

YUMMY CHOCOLATE CRUMBLE

PREP: 20 MINUTES
COOK: 45 MINUTES

Everyone thought a traditional crumble couldn't be beaten, but that's because they hadn't yet added Terry's Chocolate Orange. Give it a whirl — you won't be able to have just one crum-bowl!

FOR THE FILLING

1kg DESSERT APPLES OR RIPE PEARS, PEELED, CORED AND CUBED

50g SOFT LIGHT BROWN SUGAR

GRATED ZEST AND JUICE OF 1 ORANGE

50g DARK OR MILK TERRY'S CHOCOLATE ORANGE SEGMENTS, CHOPPED

FOR THE CRUMBLE

85g BUTTER, CHILLED AND DICED, PLUS EXTRA FOR GREASING

125g PLAIN FLOUR

60g SOFT LIGHT BROWN SUGAR

50g FLAKED ALMONDS OR CHOPPED HAZELNUTS

50g DARK OR MILK TERRY'S CHOCOLATE ORANGE SEGMENTS, CHOPPED

1. Preheat the oven to 190°C/170°C fan/gas mark 5. Lightly butter a large baking dish.

2. Put the apples or pears, sugar, orange zest and juice and chocolate in the baking dish and toss gently.

3. Make the nutty crumble: use your fingertips to rub the butter into the flour in a large bowl. When it resembles breadcrumbs, stir in the sugar, nuts and chocolate. Add 2–3 teaspoons cold water and gently stir in.

4. Cover the fruit mixture with the crumble and bake in the oven for 45 minutes, or until crisp and golden brown on top with the fruit juices bubbling through.

5. Serve warm with cream, crème fraîche, ice cream or custard.

TRY THIS

DEPENDING ON THE SEASON OR YOUR TASTES, TRY BLACKBERRIES OR GREENGAGES IN THE FRUITY FILLING, OR FLAVOUR THE FRUIT WITH GROUND CINNAMON, GINGER OR CLOVES. FOR A DIFFERENT-TEXTURED CRUMBLE, TRY STIRRING ROLLED OATS OR GROUND ALMONDS INTO THE CRUMBLE MIXTURE. MORE PLEASE!

NUTTY ORANGE PECAN TART

Crispy and creamy, this beautiful tart is just the thing for an elegant dessert. No one's ever been able to keep one around long enough to check how long it will keep for!

30g BUTTER, PLUS EXTRA FOR GREASING

500g READY-TO-ROLL PUFF PASTRY

FLOUR, FOR DUSTING

200ml GOLDEN SYRUP

30g SOFT LIGHT BROWN SUGAR

85g DARK TERRY'S CHOCOLATE ORANGE SEGMENTS, PLUS EXTRA FOR DECORATING

3 MEDIUM FREE-RANGE EGGS, BEATEN

A FEW DROPS OF VANILLA EXTRACT

175g PECAN HALVES

1. Preheat the oven to 220°C/200°C fan/gas mark 7. Lightly butter a rectangular baking tray or Swiss roll tin, about 38 × 27cm. Don't worry if the tin is slightly smaller – you can just fold the edges of the pastry over to create a thicker crust.

2. Roll out the pastry to a large rectangle on a work surface dusted with flour. Transfer it to the buttered baking tray or tin, pressing the edges up around the sides to form a crust. Prick the base lightly with a fork several times.

3. Bake in the oven for 15–20 minutes until risen and golden brown. Remove from the oven and reduce the temperature to 170°C/150°C fan/gas mark 3.

4. Meanwhile, heat the golden syrup, butter and sugar in a pan set over a medium heat, stirring until the butter melts. Remove from the heat and set aside to cool slightly.

5. Melt the Dark Terry's Chocolate Orange segments (see page 12). Allow to cool a little before stirring into the syrup mixture.

6. Beat the eggs and vanilla in a bowl and then stir in the cooled chocolate syrup mixture. Stir in the pecans, distributing them evenly throughout, and pour into the baked pastry case.

7. Bake in the oven for 20 minutes, or until set. Allow to cool slightly, then cut into slices and serve with vanilla ice cream or cream.

DELECTABLE DOUBLE CHEESECAKE

PREP: 35 MINUTES
CHILL: 6–8 HOURS

This creamy cheesecake tastes so good – rich and cool and chocolatey! When you're hosting, you can make this the day before and keep it in the fridge, and it's so easy – no baking at all.

300g DIGESTIVES
125g BUTTER, DICED
200g DARK OR MILK TERRY'S CHOCOLATE ORANGE SEGMENTS
200g CREAM CHEESE
30g ICING SUGAR
200ml DOUBLE CREAM
TERRY'S CHOCOLATE ORANGE SEGMENTS AND ORANGE ZEST SLIVERS, TO DECORATE

TRY THIS

FOR SOMETHING A LITTLE BIT SPECIAL, ADD 2 TABLESPOONS OF COCOA POWDER TO THE CRUSHED BISCUITS AND BUTTER, AND STIR SOME GRATED ORANGE ZEST INTO THE CREAM CHEESE MIXTURE.

1. Make the biscuit base: put the digestives in a ziplock bag and bash with a rolling pin until you have fine crumbs. Alternatively, pulse them in a food processor.

2. Melt the butter in a pan set over a low heat and then stir in the biscuit crumbs. Use the mixture to line the base and sides of a 20cm loose-bottomed flan tin, pressing down firmly. Chill in the fridge for 45 minutes to firm up.

3. Melt the Terry's Chocolate Orange segments (see page 12). Set aside to cool a little.

4. Using a hand-held electric whisk, beat the cream cheese and icing sugar together in a large bowl. In another bowl, whisk the cream until it stands in soft peaks.

5. Gently stir the cooled melted chocolate into the whipped cream, distributing it throughout. Fold into the cream cheese mixture and then whisk until thickened and smooth.

6. Spoon over the biscuit base, smoothing the top. Chill in the fridge for 6–8 hours, or overnight, until the cheesecake is set.

7. Decorate the top with Terry's Chocolate Orange segments and orange zest. Serve cut into slices. The cheesecake will keep well in the fridge for 2 days.

PREP: 15 MINUTES
FREEZE: 6–8 HOURS

OOH SAUCY
ICE-CREAM PUDDING

A gorgeous ice cream served with creamy chocolate sauce and a sprinkle of crunchy nuts – an extravagant dessert for a special occasion, or an excuse to crack out the ice-cream scoop on a weeknight? (As always, take special care when melting and handling white chocolate to ensure that it does not separate.)

175g WHITE TERRY'S CHOCOLATE ORANGE SEGMENTS

400ml DOUBLE CREAM

300ml CONDENSED MILK

1 tsp VANILLA EXTRACT

1 QUANTITY DARK TERRY'S CHOCOLATE ORANGE SAUCE (SEE PAGE 16), FOR DRIZZLING

CHOPPED NUTS, e.g. HAZELNUTS OR PISTACHIOS, FOR SPRINKLING

1. Melt the White Terry's Chocolate Orange segments (see page 12). Set aside to cool a little.

2. Using a hand-held electric whisk, beat the cream, condensed milk and vanilla until the mixture starts to thicken and become mousse-like, and the beaters leave a trail when you lift them out of the mixture. Gently fold in the melted chocolate with a spoon or spatula until smooth.

3. Pour into a large freezerproof container and cover with a lid. Freeze for 6–8 hours or overnight until the ice cream is firm. This will keep well in the freezer for up to 2 months.

4. Remove the ice cream from the freezer at least 10 minutes before serving. This makes it easier to scoop. Serve drizzled with Dark Terry's Chocolate Orange Sauce and a sprinkle of nuts.

TRY THIS

IF YOU'D LIKE EVEN MORE ORANGE FLAVOUR, ADD SOME GRATED ORANGE ZEST, OR SWAP THE VANILLA FOR ORANGE EXTRACT FOR SOME EXTRA ZING! YOU COULD ALSO TRY ADDING SOME CHOPPED DARK OR MILK TERRY'S CHOCOLATE ORANGE INTO THE MIXTURE JUST BEFORE FREEZING, THEN SERVING WITH FRESH SEASONAL BERRIES OR PURÉED RASPBERRIES.

SERVES 6

PREP: 15 MINUTES
FREEZE: 6–8 HOURS

TERRY'S CHOCOLATE ORANGE ICE CREAM

Chocolate Orange ice cream isn't just for the summer! This is one of the easiest no-churn ice creams you'll ever make, and you don't even need an ice-cream maker — just a few basic kitchen items to bring this classic treat to life.

150g DARK TERRY'S CHOCOLATE ORANGE SEGMENTS

400ml DOUBLE CREAM

300ml CONDENSED MILK

A FEW DROPS OF VANILLA EXTRACT

2 tbsp COCOA POWDER, SIFTED

CHOPPED OR GRATED TERRY'S CHOCOLATE ORANGE, FOR SPRINKLING

1. Melt the Terry's Chocolate Orange segments (see page 12). Allow to cool a little.

2. Using a hand-held electric whisk, beat the cream, condensed milk and vanilla until the mixture starts to thicken and become mousse-like, and the beaters leave a trail when you lift them out of the mixture.

3. Gently fold in the melted chocolate and cocoa powder with a spoon or spatula until the mixture is evenly coloured.

4. Pour into a large freezerproof container and cover with a lid. Freeze for 6–8 hours or overnight until the ice cream is firm. This will keep well in the freezer for up to 2 months.

5. Remove the ice cream from the freezer at least 10 minutes before serving (this makes it easier to scoop). Serve sprinkled with chopped or grated Chocolate Orange. Creamy, orangey, chocolatey – the best ice cream for any occasion.

COOL & CREAMY ICE-CREAM CAKE

The best treat you could give a chocoholic ice-cream lover, this is one of the easiest and quickest desserts you'll ever make. As it's also easy to make in advance and store in the freezer for up to a week, it's perfect for large gatherings where people like ice cream (that's every large gathering).

PREP: 20 MINUTES
FREEZE: OVERNIGHT

½ QUANTITY WHITE TERRY'S CHOCOLATE ORANGE ICE CREAM (SEE PAGE 93), SLIGHTLY SOFTENED

200g CHOCOLATE CHIP COOKIES, CHOPPED

½ QUANTITY TERRY'S CHOCOLATE ORANGE ICE CREAM (SEE PAGE 94), SLIGHTLY SOFTENED

500ml VANILLA ICE CREAM

DIVINE CHRISTMAS TRUFFLES (SEE PAGE 33) OR DARK CHOCOLATE CURLS, TO DECORATE

1. Line the base of a 23cm loose-bottomed springform cake tin with baking parchment.

2. Transfer the White Terry's Chocolate Orange Ice Cream to the tin and spread it out with a palette knife, smoothing and levelling the top. Sprinkle half of the chopped cookies over the top.

3. Cover with a layer of the Terry's Chocolate Orange Ice Cream and the remaining chopped cookies. Top with the vanilla ice cream, smoothing and levelling the surface.

4. Cover the tin and place in the freezer overnight until frozen hard.

5. Remove from the freezer at least 15 minutes before serving and run a thin-bladed knife around the edge of the tin before unclipping the sides. Carefully ease the bottom of the ice-cream cake off the base of the tin and slide the cake on to a large serving plate.

6. Decorate the top with Terry's Chocolate Orange Truffles or chocolate curls and serve cut into slices, dipping the knife into hot water to make it easier to cut.

SIMPLE SCRUMMY TART

PREP: 20 MINUTES
CHILL: 1½ HOURS

This wonderfully rich and chocolatey tart is so simple that even a complete novice can make it (try it, and you'll see). Serve with a dollop of whipped cream or crème fraîche to complete the experience.

FOR THE BISCUIT BASE
300g GINGERNUT BISCUITS
100g BUTTER, DICED
A PINCH OF SEA SALT

FOR THE TART FILLING
2 DARK TERRY'S CHOCOLATE ORANGES
250ml DOUBLE CREAM
2 tbsp CASTER SUGAR
75g BUTTER
75ml MILK

TO DECORATE
GRATED ORANGE ZEST
MILK TERRY'S CHOCOLATE ORANGE SEGMENTS (OPTIONAL)

1. Make the biscuit base: put the gingernut biscuits in a ziplock bag and bash with a rolling pin until you have fine crumbs. Alternatively, pulse them in a food processor.

2. Melt the butter in a pan set over a low heat and then stir in the biscuit crumbs and salt. Use the mixture to line the base and sides of a 23cm loose-bottomed flan tin, pressing down firmly. Chill in the fridge for 45 minutes to firm up while you make the filling.

3. Break the Terry's Chocolate Oranges into segments and then melt (see page 12). Set aside to cool a little.

4. Put the cream and sugar in a pan set over a medium heat. Stir until the sugar dissolves, then increase the heat and bring to the boil. Remove from the heat and set aside for a few minutes.

5. Gently stir in the melted chocolate and butter and then add the milk, stirring gently until smooth.

6. Pour into the biscuit base and leave in the fridge until completely cold and set (this should take about 45 minutes). Serve decorated with grated orange zest and Milk Chocolate Orange segments, if liked. This will keep well in the fridge for 3–4 days.

TRY THIS
IF YOU PREFER, YOU CAN USE DIGESTIVES INSTEAD OF GINGERNUTS, OR EVEN USE A READY-MADE PASTRY SHELL RATHER THAN A BISCUIT BASE. FOR AN EXTRA-SPECIAL TWIST, STIR A TABLESPOON OF COCOA POWDER INTO THE CRUMB AND MELTED BUTTER MIXTURE, AND A SPLASH OF GRAND MARNIER OR COINTREAU ORANGE LIQUEUR INTO THE FILLING. EASY, RIGHT?

QUICK TASTY TRIFLE

This recipe is a bit of a cheerful cheat as it uses ready-made supermarket custard, so it's the perfect treat for last-minute guests. And don't worry too much about the custard not setting; this is a quick and casual dessert and the custard should stay deliciously gloopy.

180g ALMOND CANTUCCINI BISCUITS

300g FRESH RASPBERRIES (OR USE FROZEN AND THAWED)

JUICE OF 1 LARGE ORANGE

2 tbsp ORANGE LIQUEUR, e.g. COINTREAU OR GRAND MARNIER (OPTIONAL)

500g READY-MADE CUSTARD

85g DARK TERRY'S CHOCOLATE ORANGE SEGMENTS, PLUS EXTRA TO DECORATE

150ml DOUBLE CREAM

YOU WILL NEED A PIPING BAG WITH A STAR-SHAPED NOZZLE

1. Break up the biscuits roughly into smallish pieces and place them in a serving bowl. Scatter the raspberries over the top and then sprinkle with the orange juice and orange liqueur (if using).

2. Heat the custard in a pan set over a medium heat. When it's hot, remove from the heat before it boils.

3. Meanwhile, melt the Dark Terry's Chocolate Orange segments (see page 12).

4. Stir the melted chocolate into the warm custard and beat it vigorously with a spoon until it is thoroughly mixed and the custard is evenly coloured throughout. Set aside to cool before pouring over the raspberries.

5. Use a hand-held electric whisk to whip the cream until it stands in stiff peaks. Spoon into a piping bag fitted with a star-shaped nozzle and pipe rosettes around the top of the trifle. Grate over some chocolate, add a few segments and chill in the fridge until ready to serve, although you can eat this straight away. If making this in advance, it will keep well in the fridge for a couple of days.

TRY THIS
FOR A BONUS CHOCOLATE TREAT, USE CHOCOLATE CHIP CANTUCCINI AS THE BASE OF YOUR TRIFLE AND — WHEN THEY'RE IN SEASON — ADD SOME CHOPPED PEACHES OR STRAWBERRIES WITH THE RASPBERRIES. UTTERLY DELICIOUS.

MELT-IN-THE-MIDDLE ZESTY PUDS

PREP: 10 MINUTES
COOK: 10 MINUTES

These 'Valenterry's' Day treats are best enjoyed with a glass of something orange or fizzy, whether you're on a tropical balcony or in your pyjamas watching a true-crime doc (who says romance is dead).

100g BUTTER, PLUS EXTRA FOR GREASING
1 MILK TERRY'S CHOCOLATE ORANGE
2 MEDIUM FREE-RANGE EGGS
50g CASTER SUGAR
50g PLAIN FLOUR
DOUBLE CREAM, TO SERVE

1. Preheat the oven to 200°C/180°C fan/gas mark 6 and lightly butter 4 small pudding moulds.

2. Lovingly smash the Milk Terry's Chocolate Orange, setting aside 4 segments. Add the remaining chocolate to a pan with the butter and melt over a low heat.

3. Whisk together the eggs and sugar in a bowl until combined and then pour in the melted chocolate. Stir, then gradually add the flour, ensuring there are no lumps.

4. Divide the mixture between the 4 moulds and place in the oven for 10 minutes.

5. For extra Valentine's points, clean up while you wait (honestly, it's worth it). Take your puddings out and allow to rest for a minute or two.

6. Turn out the puddings on to a plate, with fingers crossed for a melty molten middle. Top each with a dollop of whipped cream and a Terry's Chocolate Orange segment and serve.

BRUNCH

The greatest meal ever invented, brunch is the perfect excuse to smash a Terry's Chocolate Orange and begin your day with a chocolatey bang. From quick and simple healthier options to full-on weekend-level indulgence, there's a muffin for every morning person and a pancake for every palate.

OUTSTANDING OVERNIGHT OATS

PREP: 15 MINUTES
CHILL: OVERNIGHT

If you're more of a yawner than an early bird first thing, these overnight oats are a great solution. Prep them the night before and leave in the fridge for the flavours to emerge and the oats to plump up. When it's time for breakfast, just add your favourite healthy topping and devour!

500g 0% FAT GREEK YOGHURT

120ml UNSWEETENED ALMOND OR SOYA MILK

12 tbsp ROLLED OR PORRIDGE OATS

1 tbsp COCOA POWDER

GRATED ZEST OF 1 ORANGE

1 tbsp MAPLE SYRUP OR CLEAR HONEY

50g DARK OR MILK TERRY'S CHOCOLATE ORANGE, GRATED, PLUS EXTRA FOR SPRINKLING

1 ORANGE, PEELED, SLICED AND CUT INTO QUARTERS

2 tbsp TOASTED FLAKED ALMONDS

1. Put the yoghurt, milk, oats, cocoa powder, orange zest, maple syrup or honey and grated Chocolate Orange in a bowl and mix well.

2. Pour into 4 serving bowls or containers, then cover and leave in the fridge overnight.

3. The following morning, top with the orange segments and flaked almonds and sprinkle with grated chocolate.

TRY THIS
FOR A LITTLE MORE PROTEIN AT THE START OF YOUR DAY, ADD 2 TABLESPOONS OF CHOCOLATE PROTEIN POWDER, AND GET SOME EXTRA VITAMINS WITH A TOPPING OF RASPBERRIES AND BLUEBERRIES. IF YOU'D LIKE AN EVEN BIGGER CHOCOLATE HIT (AND WHY NOT?) USE CHOCOLATE ALMOND MILK.

TREAT YOURSELF BREAKFAST PANCAKES

Good morning! Time to wake up with some delicious chocolate pancakes. They're super-easy and ready to eat in 20 minutes — everyone who makes it to the table in time will love them.

100g DARK OR MILK
   TERRY'S CHOCOLATE
   ORANGE SEGMENTS
2 LARGE FREE-RANGE EGGS
220ml SEMI-SKIMMED MILK
5 tbsp VEGETABLE OIL, PLUS
   EXTRA FOR COOKING
160g PLAIN FLOUR
30g COCOA POWDER
2 tsp BAKING POWDER
1 tbsp CASTER SUGAR
½ tsp SALT
GREEK YOGHURT AND FRESH
   BERRIES, TO SERVE

1. Chop the Terry's Chocolate Orange segments into small chunks and set aside.

2. Break the eggs into a bowl, then beat in the milk and oil until well blended.

3. Sift the flour, cocoa and baking powder into a larger bowl and stir in the sugar and salt. Make a well in the centre and pour in the beaten egg mixture. Stir gently until everything is well combined and you have a smooth batter. Gently stir in the Chocolate Orange chunks, taking care not to overmix.

4. Lightly brush a large frying pan with oil and set over a medium–high heat. When it's hot, drop 3 or 4 tablespoons of batter into the pan, leaving plenty of space in between them. When bubbles appear on the surface after 1–2 minutes, flip the pancakes over and cook for 1–2 minutes until set and browned underneath. Remove and keep warm while you cook the rest of the pancakes in the same way.

5. Serve the pancakes piping hot, with some Greek yoghurt and fresh berries.

TRY THIS
FOR EXTRA ORANGE FLAVOUR AT THE START OF THE DAY, ADD SOME GRATED ORANGE ZEST OR A TEASPOON OF MARMALADE TO THE PANCAKE BATTER.

THE BEST BREAKFAST MUFFINS

Bake them at the weekend or the night before, and these juicy and fruity muffins will stay moist and delicious for up to three days. Take one on your commute, or pack one up for a mid-morning snack to make onlookers envious.

100g DARK TERRY'S CHOCOLATE ORANGE SEGMENTS
100g ROLLED OATS
200g PLAIN FLOUR
2 tbsp COCOA POWDER
2 tsp BAKING POWDER
½ tsp BICARBONATE OF SODA
¼ tsp SALT
100g SOFT LIGHT BROWN SUGAR
2 RIPE MEDIUM BANANAS
2 LARGE FREE-RANGE EGGS, BEATEN
60g BUTTER, MELTED
50g WALNUTS, CHOPPED
2–4 tbsp MILK
100g BLUEBERRIES

1. Preheat the oven to 180°C/160°C fan/gas mark 4. Line a 12-hole muffin tin with paper cases.

2. Chop the Terry's Chocolate Orange segments into small chunks and set aside.

3. In a large bowl, mix together the oats, flour, cocoa powder, baking powder, bicarbonate of soda, salt and sugar. Make a well in the centre.

4. Roughly mash the banana with a fork and mix with the beaten eggs and melted butter. Add to the oat mixture, then fold through gently with a metal spoon until everything is just combined. Stir in the Terry's Chocolate Orange chunks and nuts, taking care not to overmix. If the mixture is very thick, loosen it gently with a little milk.

5. Gently fold in the blueberries, distributing them throughout the mixture, and divide between the paper cases.

6. Bake in the oven for 20 minutes, or until the muffins are slightly risen and golden brown. To test whether they are cooked, insert a skewer into the centre – it should come out clean.

7. Cool on a wire rack before serving warm or cold. The muffins store well in an airtight container for 3 days.

FRENCH TOAST SANDWICHES

Sing it from the rooftops: French toast! It's delicious, filling and worth getting out of bed for. Let's leave the classic version behind and really commit to this thing by sandwiching the slices together with chocolate, to transform them into a truly celebratory start to your day.

3 MEDIUM FREE-RANGE
   EGGS
180ml MILK
1 tbsp CASTER SUGAR
8 MEDIUM SLICES OF
   WHITE BREAD
25g UNSALTED BUTTER
100g DARK OR MILK TERRY'S
   CHOCOLATE ORANGE
   SEGMENTS, CHOPPED
   INTO SMALL PIECES
ICING SUGAR OR GROUND
   CINNAMON, FOR DUSTING
STRAWBERRIES, TO SERVE
   (OPTIONAL)

1. Whisk together the eggs, milk and sugar in a bowl, then pour into a large shallow dish.

2. Quickly dip 2 bread slices into the egg mixture, turning them to coat on both sides.

3. Meanwhile, heat the butter in a large non-stick frying pan set over a medium heat.

4. Place the soaked bread slices in the pan and sprinkle half the chopped chocolate over them. Soak another 2 bread slices and place them on top of the chocolate covered ones in the pan to make 2 'sandwiches'.

5. Cook for 2–3 minutes until golden brown underneath, then, using a spatula, carefully flip them over and cook the other side until golden and the chocolate filling has melted. Keep warm while you cook the remaining French toast in the same way.

6. Cut each 'sandwich' in half diagonally and dust with icing sugar or cinnamon. Serve with fresh strawberries, if you like.

PREP: 5 MINUTES
COOK: 8 MINUTES

CHOCOLATE-PACKED PORRIDGE

Brrrrr! Nothing is better on a cold day than a bowl of healthy, warming porridge. A great source of protein and with a low GI, it's brilliant for stopping those elevenses hunger pangs. But for all that, it can be a bit … bland. So we've added some yummy chocolate. You're welcome!

85g PORRIDGE OATS

480ml WATER

480ml OAT MILK OR ALMOND MILK (OR USE DAIRY MILK)

A PINCH OF SALT

1 tbsp COCOA POWDER

GRATED ZEST OF 1 ORANGE

CASTER SUGAR, MAPLE SYRUP OR SWEETENER, TO TASTE

50g DARK TERRY'S CHOCOLATE ORANGE SEGMENTS, CHOPPED INTO SMALL CHUNKS

2 tbsp 0% FAT GREEK YOGHURT OR REDUCED-FAT CRÈME FRAÎCHE

2 tbsp TOASTED MIXED SEEDS, e.g. SUNFLOWER, PUMPKIN, SESAME, CHIA

1. Put the oats, water and milk in a non-stick pan. Add the salt, cocoa powder and orange zest and stir well with a wooden spoon.

2. Place over a high heat and bring to the boil, stirring frequently. When the porridge starts to boil and thicken, reduce the heat to low and cook for 4–5 minutes until thick and creamy.

3. Sweeten to taste and divide the porridge between 2 serving bowls. Gently stir in the chocolate chunks, so they start to melt slightly into the porridge.

4. Serve topped with yoghurt or crème fraîche and a sprinkle of mixed seeds.

TRY THIS
IF YOU WANT A PROTEIN BOOST FIRST THING, REPLACE THE COCOA POWDER WITH 1–2 TABLESPOONS OF CHOCOLATE PROTEIN POWDER, OR IF MORNING IS YOUR TIME TO TREAT YOURSELF, LEAVE THE COCOA OUT AND ADD CHOPPED WHITE TERRY'S CHOCOLATE ORANGE SEGMENTS JUST BEFORE SERVING. TOP YOUR DELICIOUS WARM BOWL WITH FRESH BERRIES, POACHED PEARS OR RHUBARB. NOW YOU'RE GOOD TO GO!

PREP: 10 MINUTES
COOK: 20–25 MINUTES

ZESTY GRANOLA

This granola is the best of the best. There's enough here for four servings, but it's easy to double the quantities for a bigger batch, as it keeps well stored in an airtight container for up to 2 weeks (and there's never a bad time for some granola).

2 tbsp COCONUT OIL
3 tbsp MAPLE SYRUP
100g ROLLED OATS
40g CHOPPED HAZELNUTS
40g CHOPPED ALMONDS
25g SUNFLOWER SEEDS
25g PUMPKIN SEEDS
2 tbsp SESAME SEEDS
50g RAISINS
1 tbsp COCOA POWDER
½ tsp GROUND CINNAMON
A GOOD PINCH OF SEA SALT
75g DARK, MILK OR WHITE TERRY'S CHOCOLATE ORANGE SEGMENTS, CHOPPED INTO SMALL PIECES

TO SERVE
FRESH BERRIES, CHOPPED FRUIT, YOGHURT, ALMOND BUTTER, MILK
HONEY OR MAPLE SYRUP, FOR DRIZZLING

1. Preheat the oven to 170°C/150°C fan/gas mark 3. Line a large baking tray with baking parchment.

2. Heat the coconut oil and maple syrup in a pan set over a low heat. When the coconut oil melts, stir in the oats, nuts, seeds, raisins, cocoa powder, cinnamon and sea salt. Make sure that everything is well coated.

3. Spread the mixture out evenly in a thin layer on the lined baking tray and bake in the oven for 15–20 minutes, stirring once or twice, until golden brown and crisp.

4. Leave to cool; when it is cold, stir in the Terry's Chocolate Orange pieces and transfer to an airtight container.

5. Serve the granola with the topping and drizzle of your choice.

TRY THIS
TO MIX THINGS UP A LITTLE, VARY THE NUTS: TRY WALNUTS OR PECANS, AND ADD IN SOME DRIED CRANBERRIES OR CHOPPED DRIED APRICOTS FOR A LITTLE FRUITY MORNING TREAT.

DRINKS

Look at a classic Terry's Chocolate Orange, you might not imagine that melting it down and adding a little milk of your choice would open the doors to a whole new world of chocolatey delights: lattes, hot chocolates, shakes and smoothies. Just find a glass or mug, and get making . . .

DECADENT ORANGE MILKSHAKE

PREP: 15 MINUTES

Chocolatey, thick and rich, this is possibly the best chocolate milkshake you'll ever have! Don't believe it? Just try it once . . .

75g MILK TERRY'S CHOCOLATE ORANGE SEGMENTS, CHOPPED

300ml CHILLED MILK (FULL-FAT, SEMI-SKIMMED OR SKIMMED)

4 SCOOPS OF TERRY'S CHOCOLATE ORANGE ICE CREAM (SEE PAGE 94)

WHIPPED CREAM, TO SERVE

MILK OR DARK TERRY'S CHOCOLATE ORANGE SAUCE (SEE PAGE 16), FOR DRIZZLING

1. Put the chocolate in a blender with half of the milk and pulse until the chocolate has broken down into tiny pieces. Add the remaining milk and the ice cream and blend until thick and creamy.

2. Pour into 4 tall glasses and top each milkshake with some whipped cream. Drizzle with the chocolate sauce and serve immediately.

TRY THIS

YOU CAN USE ANY GOOD-QUALITY CHOCOLATE ICE CREAM, IF YOU DON'T HAVE TERRY'S CHOCOLATE ORANGE ICE CREAM, AND DRIZZLE THE WHOLE THING WITH CHOCOLATE SYRUP OR SPRINKLE WITH GRATED TERRY'S CHOCOLATE ORANGE. *MMMMM.*

OUT OF THIS WORLD ORANGE LATTE

This isn't just a caffeine pick-me-up — this is a mouth-watering, chocolatey, creamy latte. We've used White Terry's Chocolate Orange to make these, but you could substitute Milk if you prefer. This quantity is enough to make 4 small lattes or 2 large ones (or one massive one, depending on how your day is going). *See photo on previous page.*

PREP: 15 MINUTES

400ml SEMI-SKIMMED MILK
2 tbsp DOUBLE CREAM
A FEW DROPS OF VANILLA EXTRACT
1 tbsp SUGAR
50g WHITE TERRY'S CHOCOLATE ORANGE SEGMENTS, CHOPPED
4 SHOTS ESPRESSO (OR 2 PODS)
WHIPPED CREAM AND GRATED TERRY'S CHOCOLATE ORANGE, TO SERVE

1. Heat the milk, cream and vanilla extract in a pan set over a medium-high heat. Stir in the sugar and chocolate, stirring until it melts. Whisk or froth with a hand-held electric frother.

2. Pour the espresso into 4 cups or 2 mugs. Pour the frothed milk slowly and steadily from a relatively high position into the cups. The milk should pour first with the froth at the end as you lower the jug towards the cup.

3. Top with whipped cream and grated chocolate. Serve immediately and enjoy!

TIP: If you don't have an espresso machine or pot, you can still enjoy these divine drinks! Just use a cafetière, or even strong instant coffee, and drizzle with some chocolate or caramel syrup before serving.

**SERVES
2**

PREP: 10 MINUTES

COMFORTING
HOT CHOCOLATE

This is as good as it gets: wonderfully creamy, thick and smooth, and great when you need something hot and comforting in winter (or in spring, autumn or even summer – you know what British weather is like). For a white hot chocolate drink, just substitute White Terry's Chocolate Orange for the Dark.

300ml MILK
100ml DOUBLE CREAM
A LONG SLIVER OF ORANGE
    PEEL
100g DARK TERRY'S
    CHOCOLATE ORANGE
    SEGMENTS, CHOPPED
SUGAR, TO TASTE
    (OPTIONAL)

1. Put the milk and cream in a pan with the orange peel and set over a low heat, stirring well.

2. When it's hot, remove the orange peel and add the chocolate. Stir gently until the chocolate melts and the mixture thickens. It should be smooth, rich and creamy.

3. Add sugar (if using) to taste and pour into 2 mugs. Serve immediately.

TRY THIS
IF YOU DESERVE MORE THAN JUST THE BEST HOT CHOCOLATE EVER, TOP YOURS WITH MOUNDS OF WHIPPED CREAM, A SPRINKLE OF GRATED CHOCOLATE, TERRY'S CHOCOLATE ORANGE SEGMENTS OR MINI MARSHMALLOWS. OR – WHY NOT? – ALL FOUR . . .

**SERVES
2**

SMOOTH'N'CHOCOLATEY SMOOTHIE

Great for breakfast, a snack or even post-workout, this is ideal for when you're feeling peckish and in need of something sweet. The protein powder and milk give this tasty drink a nutritious kick.

PREP: 15 MINUTES

1 LARGE FROZEN BANANA,
   CUT INTO CHUNKS
2 SCOOPS OF TERRY'S
   CHOCOLATE ORANGE
   ICE CREAM (SEE
   PAGE 94)
300ml MILK OR
   DAIRY-FREE MILK
2 tbsp CHOCOLATE
   PROTEIN POWDER

FOR THE TOPPING
GRATED TERRY'S
   CHOCOLATE ORANGE
SHAVED OR DESICCATED
   COCONUT

1. Blitz the frozen banana, ice cream, milk and protein powder in a blender until smooth.

2. Divide the mixture between 2 glasses and sprinkle with the grated chocolate and coconut. Serve immediately.

TRY THIS
IF THERE'S NOT ENOUGH CHOCOLATE HIT IN THERE, ADD SOME EXTRA COCOA POWDER, THEN TOP WITH SOME CHOPPED TERRY'S CHOCOLATE ORANGE AND A FEW BLUEBERRIES OR RASPBERRIES. IT'S WORTH GETTING UP WHEN A SMOOTHIE IS THIS GOOD!

118

SERVES 2

PREP: 15 MINUTES

HUG-IN-A-MUG
WHITE HOT CHOCOLATE

Exotic and rich, this creamy hot chocolate uses coconut milk — but you can use any milk (dairy, nut or oat) and either full-fat or reduced-fat coconut milk. Once you taste it, you'll be coconutty for this combo.

150ml MILK
150ml TINNED COCONUT MILK
50g WHITE TERRY'S CHOCOLATE ORANGE SEGMENTS, CHOPPED
GRATED DARK TERRY'S CHOCOLATE ORANGE AND TOASTED COCONUT FLAKES, FOR SPRINKLING

1. Heat the milk and coconut milk in a pan set over a medium heat, stirring occasionally.

2. Take the pan off the heat and add the chopped chocolate, stirring gently until it melts.

3. Place the pan back over a low–medium heat and heat through gently.

4. Pour into 2 mugs and sprinkle with grated chocolate and coconut flakes.

TRY THIS
ON A COLD DAY WITH FRIENDS, WHY NOT ADD A LITTLE COCONUT RUM, LIKE MALIBU? OR FOR CHILDREN (OF ANY AGE), TOP THIS WARMING DRINK WITH WHIPPED CREAM AND DUST WITH GROUND CINNAMON.

HarperCollins*Publishers*
1 London Bridge Street
London SE1 9GF

www.harpercollins.co.uk

HarperCollins*Publishers*
1st Floor, Watermarque Building, Ringsend Road
Dublin 4, Ireland

First published by HarperCollins*Publishers* 2022

10 9 8 7 6 5 4 3 2 1

Recipes created by Heather Thomas and Terry's
Additional content by Anne-Sophie and Paul Sanchez, Ma Jolie Food
Food styling by Kim Morphew
Prop styling by Lydia Brun

A catalogue record for this book is available from the British Library

ISBN 978-0-00-850324-6

Printed and bound in Latvia

MIX
Paper from
responsible sources
FSC™ C007454